Alexander D. Anderson

The Silver Country

Or, the great Southwest. A review of the mineral and other wealth, the attractions and material development of the former kingdom of New Spain, comprising Mexico and the Mexican cessions to the United States in 1848 and 1853

Alexander D. Anderson

The Silver Country
Or, the great Southwest. A review of the mineral and other wealth, the attractions and material development of the former kingdom of New Spain, comprising Mexico and the Mexican cessions to the United States in 1848 and 1853

ISBN/EAN: 9783337172299

Printed in Europe, USA, Canada, Australia, Japan

Cover: Foto ©ninafisch / pixelio.de

More available books at **www.hansebooks.com**

THE
SILVER COUNTRY

OR

THE GREAT SOUTHWEST

A REVIEW OF THE MINERAL AND OTHER WEALTH, THE
ATTRACTIONS AND MATERIAL DEVELOPMENT OF THE
FORMER KINGDOM OF NEW SPAIN, COMPRISING
MEXICO AND THE MEXICAN CESSIONS
TO THE UNITED STATES IN
1848 AND 1853

BY

ALEX. D. ANDERSON

———

NEW YORK
G. P. PUTNAM'S SONS
182 FIFTH AVENUE
1877

PREFACE.

No work on New Spain, considered as a whole, has been published since the close of the war with Mexico, when half of the territory known by that name was acquired by the United States; and, on the subject of its resources, no work since Ward's "Mexico," issued in 1827. That valuable book was published in London, is little known in this country, and is to be found in very few of our public libraries. So, for all practical purposes, Baron Humboldt's "Political Essay on New Spain," translated into English, and published in London in 1822, is the latest authority. Books on individual States or Territories of the Southwest are, however, abundant. But a general or more comprehensive review seems to be needed for business and other purposes.

The Southwest, in the early part of the sixteenth century, because of its mineral wealth and luxuries, excited the admiration of the whole world. It is once more coming into great prominence, and is destined to play a leading part on the stage of public affairs, both national and international. The advance of internal improvements through its territory, and the beginning of a new era of material development, is reuniting New Spain in an industrial and commercial sense, and makes necessary a grouping together of local facts and statistics into a general work. Such a combination of statistics gives wonderful results, for Mexico, prolific in treasures, golden California, and silver Nevada come within its limits.

New Spain seems to be the natural and most convenient territorial basis for a book, for the reason that it was, for three hundred years, from 1521, when Cortez and his soldiers accomplished the conquest, until 1821, when Mexico declared her independence, ruled by the Spaniards, who were very prolific writers, and who in their many histories observed the same territorial limits. Again, the country, as a whole, is very uniform in its characteristics, such as general prevalence of silver, high table-lands, ancient history prior to the Spanish rule, and in many other respects.

This is a book of facts, not theories. It describes the land of silver, and shows that the Southwest is producing, each year, two-thirds of the silver of the whole world; but it does not attempt to discuss the merits of a double standard of gold and silver. It treats of railways generally, and gives facts and figures showing how these great civilizers have neglected the Southwest; but it does not advocate any individual enterprise. It freely expresses its admiration for undeveloped Mexico; but it does not join in any cry for another conquest, except so far as the future conquest may consist of the advance of railways, a thrifty civilization in place of the inertia of the present lethargic races, of commerce and the arts of peace, all of which will stimulate the material prosperity of both Republics. It does not profess to be a full review of the varied riches and attractions of the Southwest, as such a review would require several large volumes. But it does claim to be accurate, and the authorities are freely cited, in legal brief style, to confirm the accuracy of all statements and statistics. Nature was so profusely liberal in the endowment of this portion of the earth's surface, that facts about the riches of the Southwest furnish the writer with abundant material, and it is unnecessary to draw on the imagination to make out a case.

Much time and labor have been spent in the search for and examination of the various books composing the list in the chapter on Authorities; and it is believed that chapter will be serviceable to the reader, for the reason that of the one hundred and twenty-nine volumes on Old Mexico, about half, and that the best half, were published in London, and have a very limited circulation in this country.

The author hopes that the facts and figures in the following pages will act as an appetizer for more, and will attract the attention of the reader to the rich feast of information which the Spanish, English, and American discoverers, travelers, and historians have prepared in their many volumes.

The elevations of the southern or Mexican half of New Spain, as given in the accompanying map, are from an hypsometric map in Geiger's "Peep at Mexico," published at London in 1874. For the illustration of the elevations of the northern half of New Spain (now a portion of the United States) the author is indebted to W. H. Holmes, Esq., of Prof. Hayden's Survey, who prepared the map, to correspond to that of Mexico, from data contained in the detailed and elaborate hypsometric map issued by that Survey during the present year.

The railway lines are from recent official and other reliable sources.

ALEX. D. ANDERSON.

WASHINGTON, D. C., *October*, 1877.

CONTENTS.

CHAPTER I.

DEFINITION AND DESCRIPTIVE NOTES.

Definition, 11 — Bounderies, 15 — Area and comparisons, 19 — Table-lands and elevations, 21 — Its remarkable situation, 25.

CHAPTER II.

ITS WEALTH IN SILVER AND GOLD.

The treasures of the Toltecs and Aztecs........................ 29
Working of the mines by the Toltecs and Aztecs................ 36
Product of silver and gold of Mexico, 1521-1804................ 39
Product of silver and gold of Mexico, 1804-1848................ 41
Product of silver and gold of Mexico, 1848-1876................ 42
Product of silver and gold of California, 1848-1876............ 43
Product of silver and gold of Nevada, 1848-1876................ 45
Product of silver and gold of Arizona, 1848-1876............... 46
Product of silver and gold of New Mexico, 1848-1876........... 47
Product of silver and gold of Utah, 1848-1876.................. 48
Product of silver and gold of Southern and Western Colorado, 1848-1876.... 49
Total product of silver and gold of the Southwest or New Spain, 1521-1876... 50

Progress of mining in the Southwest.......................... 51
Products of silver and gold of the Southwest compared with each other.. 54
Products of silver and gold of the Southwest compared with that of the world.. 58
Product of silver and gold of Mexico since 1848 compared with that of the territory ceded by her to the United States....... 59
Product of silver and gold since 1848 of the territory acquired from Mexico compared with that of the rest of the United States... 59
Silver product of the Southwest, or New Spain, compared with that of the whole world... 60
Mineral wealth of the Border States........................... 64
Present condition and wants of the mining industry............ 71
Future products of silver and gold in the Southwest........... 76

CHAPTER III.

OTHER WEALTH THAN SILVER AND GOLD.

Preliminary remarks... 79
Wheat... 81
Cotton.. 87
Indian corn... 91
Barley.. 93
Cattle.. 93
Sheep and wool.. 95
Coffee.. 96
Sugar... 98
Cochineal... 101

CONTENTS.

Silk.. 102
Quicksilver... 102
Fruits and wines.. 103
Résumé... 106

CHAPTER IV.

LUXURIES AND ATTRACTIONS.

Facilities for the acquirement of wealth................ 108
Topography and climate................................. 110
Scenery and wonders.................................... 113
Antiquities.. 118
Flowers.. 123
Fruits and wines....................................... 125
Luxurious living....................................... 126

CHAPTER V.

THE AUTHORITIES.

Preliminary.. 130
Aztec Books.. 133
Spanish histories...................................... 135
Works in English....................................... 136
Authorities on Mexico.................................. 137
Authorities on California.............................. 149
Authorities on Texas................................... 157
Authorities on New Mexico.............................. 162
Authorities on Arizona................................. 164
Authorities on South and West Colorado................. 165

Authorities on Nevada..................................... 166
Authorities on Utah....................................... 167
Authorities too general for the above territorial classification.... 168
Résumé.. 183

CHAPTER VI.

THE FOREIGN COMMERCE OF MEXICO.

Its natural course... 188
Mexico's exchanges with all countries 190
Mexico's exchanges with the United States................... 196

CHAPTER VII.

THE ADVANCE OF RAILWAYS.

The importance of national highways......................... 201
The advance of railways in the United States, and the Southwest.. 205
The advance of railways in the Southwest compared with that in other countries and the world.......................... 208
Facilities for constructing railways in the Southwest........... 212
Reasons why railways have not crossed the Southwest......... 217
A look ahead.. 218

CONCLUSION.. 219

THE SILVER COUNTRY;

OR,

THE GREAT SOUTHWEST.

CHAPTER I.

DEFINITION AND DESCRIPTIVE NOTES.

DEFINITION.

SOON after the conquest of Mexico, in 1521, by Cortez and his soldiers, the restless ambition of the Spanish stimulated them to extend the possessions of their king farther north into the present territory of New Mexico and Arizona. As early as 1530, say the historians, Nuno de Guzman, one of the leading officials of Mexico, under the crown, heard from a native Indian of cities in the north. He organized a company of soldiers, and set out for their conquest; but the expedition became disbanded on the way.* A few years later, about

---

* "The Conquest of New Mexico," by W. W. H. Davis, p. 110.

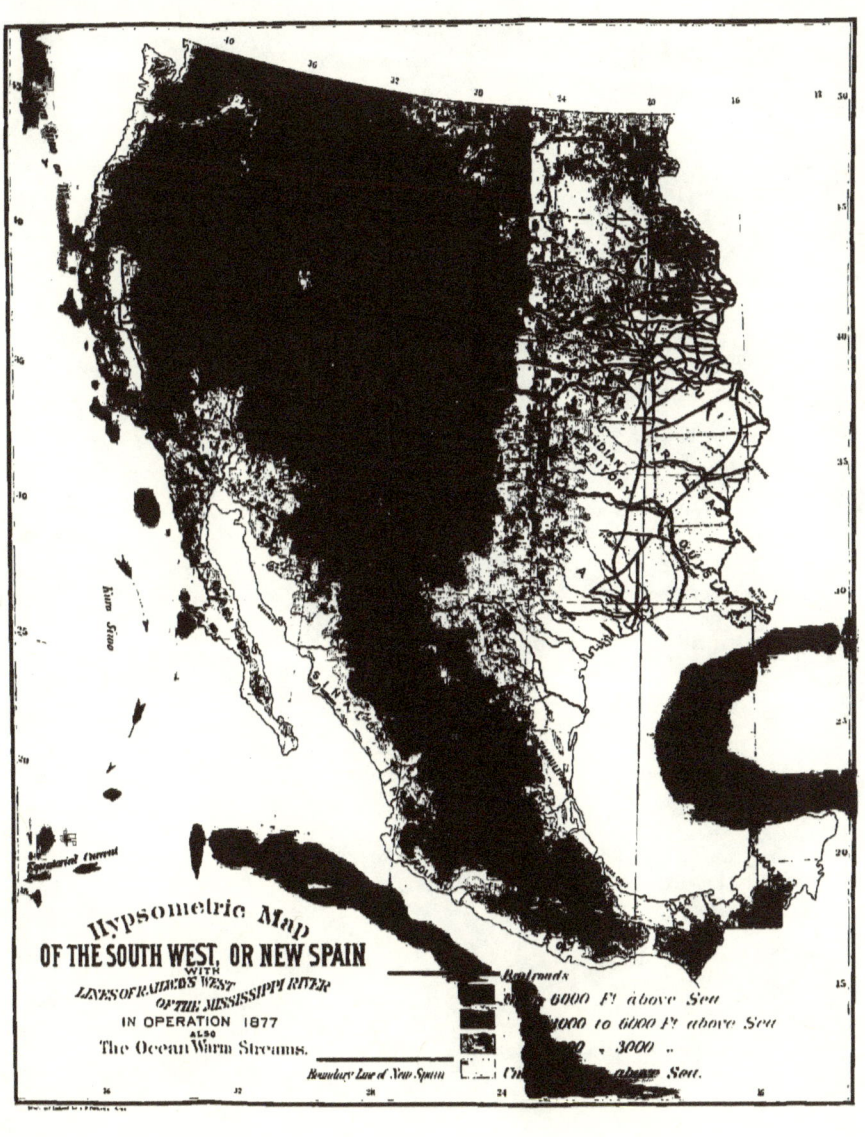

THE SILVER COUNTRY;

OR,

THE GREAT SOUTHWEST.

CHAPTER I.

DEFINITION AND DESCRIPTIVE NOTES.

DEFINITION.

SOON after the conquest of Mexico, in 1521, by Cortez and his soldiers, the restless ambition of the Spanish stimulated them to extend the possessions of their king farther north into the present territory of New Mexico and Arizona. As early as 1530, say the historians, Nuno de Guzman, one of the leading officials of Mexico, under the crown, heard from a native Indian of cities in the north. He organized a company of soldiers, and set out for their conquest; but the expedition became disbanded on the way.* A few years later, about

---

* "The Conquest of New Mexico," by W. W. H. Davis, p. 110.

1536, one Cabeza de Vaca, with a few comrades, escaping from an unfortunate Spanish expedition to Florida, crossed overland from the Gulf of Mexico, and passed through New Mexico and Arizona, on the way to Old Mexico to join their countrymen. They brought with them further reports of large cities in the north.

Marco de Niza, a Franciscan friar, was, in 1539, sent in command of an expedition to investigate the reports.* He went far enough to see, but was too cautious to enter the cities. He did not hesitate, on his return, to describe them in the most glowing terms, and immediately the Spanish love of conquest and glory knew no restraint. A well-equipped military expedition, under the lead of Don Francisco Vasquez Coronado, started in the early part of 1541, to subject the " Seven Cities of Cibola," as they were called, to the Spanish rule. They found the cities, and captured all seven, which together constituted one province. The historian of the "Conquest of New Mexico" says: "The province of Cibola contained seven villages, situated in a warm valley between high mountains; one of them took the name of the province, and another, called Muzaque, is said to have been the most populous. The houses were ordinarily four and five stories high, and some few in Muzaque were six and

---

* Idem, p. 114.

seven." * These cities were near the present city of Zuni, and near the boundary line between New Mexico and Arizona, about halfway between their northern and southern limits. After this victory Coronado and his soldiers, in their explorations of the northern country, marched through several other provinces, which together contained seventy villages or cities. The line of their march extended across nearly the whole length and breadth of Arizona and New Mexico, through Southern Colorado, and up through Kansas to its northern boundary, and back through what is now the Indian Territory.† Wherever they went they were victorious.‡ But they did not find such magnificent palaces and treasures as Cortez had found in Montezuma's Mexico. The expedition of Coronado was not at once followed up by Spanish settlements; but as early as 1591, Don Juan de Onate, with a large number of followers, went north to remain and introduce Spanish civilization § in what is now the Territory of New Mexico. Soon after others established settlements and missions in California, Arizona, and Texas.

This broad and then undefined country in the north, together with the present Republic of Mex-

---

* Idem, p. 167.   † Idem, p. 221.   ‡ Idem, p. 267.
§ See Simpson's account of the march, in Smithsonian Report for 1867.

ico, was, as early as 1522, known as New Spain, and was ruled by Spanish viceroys until Mexico threw off the Spanish yoke in 1821. It is the same country and the only portion of North America which was occupied by the civilized nations of the native races for centuries prior to the conquest. It is the portion of America oldest in European civilization. It is the same country that the Spanish historians wrote about for three centuries. It is the land that was called Mexico until the revolution in Texas caused the first loss of territory; but as Mexico continued to claim Texas until 1848, we will call it Mexico until that date. It is, then, a combination of Mexico and the territory she relinquished to the United States in 1848 by the treaty of Guadalupe Hidalgo, and by the treaty of 1853, commonly known as the Gadsden Purchase. It is, in other words, a combination of old Mexico, New Mexico, Arizona, California, Texas, Nevada, Utah, and Southern and Western Colorado. Strictly defined it is the southwest portion of North America. It is, finally, a country very uniform in its resources, characteristics, and attractions. Later events have helped to define the limits of New Spain, and as, for the purposes of this book, the Southwest and New Spain are used as interconvertible terms, we will briefly locate the lines.

BOUNDARIES.

Baron Humboldt, in his exhaustive work on New Spain (the time of his explorations being about the beginning of the present century), said: "The kingdom of New Spain, the most northern part of all Spanish America, extends from the 16th to the 38th degree of latitude." Farther on, in the same volume, he says: "We are uncertain as to the limits which ought to be assigned to New Spain to the north and east."* In 1803 the United States, by the Treaty of Paris, purchased the Province of Louisiana from France, and the southern and western boundaries of that purchase would, if they had been defined, determine the dividing line between the United States and New Spain. But the treaty was silent on that point, and not until the treaty between the United States and Spain, of February 22, 1819, was the boundary finally adjusted. This treaty was the result of lengthy correspondence and negotiations between John Quincy Adams, then Secretary of State, and Don Louis de Onis, the Spanish minister. The claims of their respective Governments were based upon the disputed limits of the early French and Spanish discoveries and settlements in the Southwest. The United States having previously pur-

---

* "Political Essay on New Spain," i. 16 and 274.

chased all of the possessions and claims of France west of the Mississippi River, took the place of France in this correspondence about the dividing line. Mr. Adams claimed that La Salle and other French explorers, who entered the Mississippi valley from Canada, on the north, had, after exploring nearly the whole length of the Mississippi, extended the possessions of France far into the southwest, or to a point within the present State of Texas. The Spanish minister opposed this claim, and maintained that the early voyages and discoveries of De Soto, Narvaez, and others, and the fact that the province of Texas was organized as early as 1690 by the viceroyalty of New Spain, gave Spain title to territory in the southwest claimed by the United States as the successor of France. The treaty was the result of these historical researches and negotiations.* The language of the treaty on the limits is as follows: "The boundary line between the two countries, west of the Mississippi, shall begin on the Gulf of Mexico, at the mouth of the river Sabine, in the sea, continuing north along the western bank of that river to the 32d degree of latitude; thence by a line due north, to the degree of latitude where it strikes the Rio Roxo of Nachitoches, or Red River; then fol-

---

* See vol. iv. "American State Papers on Foreign Affairs," pp. 468 to 478.

DEFINITION AND DESCRIPTIVE NOTES. 17

lowing the course of the Rio Roxo westward to the degree of longitude 100 west from London, and 23 from Washington; then crossing the said Red River and running thence, by a line due north, to the river Arkansas; thence following the course of the southern bank of the Arkansas to its source, in latitude 42 north; and thence by that parallel of latitude to the South Sea. The whole being as laid down in Melish's map of the United States published at Philadelphia, improved to the first of January, 1818. But if the source of the Arkansas River shall be found to fall north or south of latitude 42, then the line shall run from the said source, due south or north, as the case may be, till it meets the said parallel of latitude 42, and thence along the said parallel to the South Sea." *

A subsequent section of the treaty provided for the appointment of commissioners and surveyors to run the line, but for some reason they were not appointed. After Mexico became independent, a treaty between that Republic and the United States, in 1828, made a similar provision for commissioners and surveyors to run the line, but again was the duty under the treaty neglected.† The line is not yet definitely located, except by the language of the treaty of 1819, without a survey.

---

* 8 United States Statutes, pp. 255-6.
† Idem, p. 372.

That language is sufficiently definite, except in locating the line from the source of the Arkansas River to the 42° of north latitude, and here there may be a conflict of opinion in regard to the true source of the river. A recent drainage map of Colorado, by the surveying expedition under Prof. Hayden, shows one of the sources to be at Homestake Peak, about latitude 39° 20' north, and longitude 106° 25' west, on the dividing ridge between the waters of the Atlantic and Pacific. A boundary commission appointed to carry out the provisions of the treaty might select some other one of the small mountain streams as the true source of the Arkansas River, and thereby locate the line several miles east or west of the one running north from Homestake Peak. As the treaty of 1848 between the United States and Mexico changed the boundary line between the two Republics and placed it far in the southwest, the line through Colorado ceased to be of international importance, and for that reason was the survey neglected after the Mexican war. But as a matter of history, it is to be regretted that it was not surveyed. Possibly the investigation by the United States courts of the Spanish or Mexican land claims in Southern Colorado may again make this historical line of practical importance.

New Spain, or the Southwest, may then be said

to embrace all of the present Republic of Mexico and that portion of the United States south and west of a line from the Gulf up the course of the Sabine River to latitude 32°; thence by a line due north to the Red River; thence along the course of that river to longitude 100 west from London; thence due north to the Arkansas River; thence along that river to its source; thence due north to latitude 42°; thence along that parallel of latitude to the Pacific Ocean.

AREA AND COMPARISONS.

To the New-England reader, who is accustomed to smaller divisions of territory, it may seem an exaggeration to assert that New Spain will contain New England, territorially, twenty-five times. Yet such is the fact. The single State of Texas will contain all New England four times. It will contain Rhode Island two hundred and ten times, yet the two States are equally represented in the United States Senate. The areas, in square miles, of the six States and Territories which come wholly within the limits of the acquisitions from Mexico, and consequently wholly within that portion of New Spain now possessed by the United States, are, contrasted with the areas of the six New-England States, as follows:

Texas..............	274,356	Maine.............	35,000
California......	188,981	Vermont.........	10,212
New Mexico...	121,200	New Hampshire.	9,280
Nevada.........	104,125	Massachusetts...	7,800
Arizona.........	113,916	Connecticut.....	4,750
Utah............	84,476	Rhode Island...	1,306
Total......	887,054	Total......	68,348

Adding 80,397 for the area of the fractional parts of other States within the limits of the acquisitions, we have a total of 967,451 square miles acquired from Mexico, as against 761,640 square miles which Mexico has left. These figures combined show the area of New Spain to be 1,729,091 square miles, or a territory as large as the combined areas of England, Wales, Scotland, Ireland, France, Spain, Italy, and, to save the trouble of naming further European nations, we will add England twenty-one times more, and yet have territory enough left for several extensive cattle ranches. To contrast the new with the old, New Spain will contain the kingdom of Spain over eight times. How many times richer it is in products of silver and gold, and how much glory the crown of Spain gained, but to lose in America, will appear in subsequent pages.

TABLE-LANDS AND ELEVATIONS.

Referring again to Baron Humboldt, whose works are the standard authority on New Spain, he says of the country constituting the great interior of the Southwest between Santa Fé in New Mexico, and the city of Mexico: "We are led to ask whether in the whole world there exists any similar formation of equal extent and height (between five thousand and seven thousand feet above the level of the sea). Four-wheeled waggons can travel from Mexico to Santa Fé. The plateau whose leveling I have here described is formed solely by the broad undulating flattened crest of the chain of the Mexican Andes; it is not the swelling of a valley between two mountain chains."* Another good authority tells how a wheeled carriage could start on a table-land five thousand five hundred feet high in the State of Oajaca, a little above the Isthmus of Tehuantepec, and as far south as latitude 16° 20', and roll on without difficulty to Santa Fé in the north, a distance of above one thousand four hundred miles.†

It is safe to assert that the same carriage might find a high table-land, good roads, and an easy trip

---

* "Views of Nature," p. 209.

† Paper on Mexico in Lippincott's Gazetteer of the World.

northward into Southern Colorado, near the upper boundary of New Spain.

A French writer on Mexico, after describing some high mountain-peaks near latitude 19° north, says: "With the exception of the narrow band marked by these majestic peaks, Mexico presents a table-land stretching out far toward the north, with undulations that have no notable change of altitude save at long distances. Immense plains looking like the dry basins of ancient lakes succeed one another, separated by hills that barely rise six hundred and fifty to eight hundred feet above the general level." *

Another authority describing the Mexican Andes says: "The backs of the mountains form very elevated plateaus, or basins sufficiently uniform in height to be regarded as one continuous table-land." †

Another writer, after explaining how the great chain of mountains which enters Mexico in the south soon divides into two parts and extend northwardly on opposite sides of Mexico along the coast lines, says: "The whole of the vast tract of country between these two great arms, comprising about three-fifths of the entire surface of the empire, consists of a central table-land, called the plateau of Anahuac, elevated from six thousand to upward of

---

* "Mexico, Ancient and Modern," by Chevalier, 2d vol., p. 98.
† Paper on Mexico in American Cyclopædia.

eight thousand feet above the level of the sea. Hence, though a large portion of this plateau be within the limits of the torrid zone, it enjoys a temperate climate, inclining, indeed, more to cold than to excess of heat." *

The central portion of this remarkable table-land of Mexico is more elevated than the sides, but even they are sufficiently elevated to make the descent generally abrupt and difficult on the east and west. The same formation continues, as we go north, into that portion of New Spain lying within the limits of the United States, but near the boundary between the two republics the country is less elevated, and slopes more gradually on the east and west sides.

The whole territory of New Mexico is a continuation of the table-land extending northwardly from old Mexico, and speaking generally, may be called a gradually inclined plain. Even the Rio Grande River flowing through the middle of New Mexico is an elevated or mountain river, being at El Paso, on the southern line of the territory, 3,800 feet above the sea, at the northern line of the territory about 7,000 feet above the sea.† Gannett accounts for the 121,200 square miles of territory in New Mexico as follows: ‡

---

* Paper on Mexico in McCulloch's Geographical Dictionary.
† "List of Elevations," by Henry Gannett, Washington, 1877, p. 149.
‡ Idem, pp. 160–162.

Elevations in Feet.			Square Miles.
3,000	and	4,000	2,000
4,000	"	5,000	52,000
5,000	"	6,000	28,000
6,000	"	7,000	22,000
7,000	"	8,000	6,500
8,000	"	9,000	5,000
9,000	"	10,000	3,200
10,000	"	11,000	1,800
11,000	"	12,000	700

No wonder the people of New Mexico love their mountain home, and prefer its pure and invigorating air to the depressing fogs and heavy atmosphere of lower elevations.

The mean height of each of the six divisions, or States, of New Spain, lying wholly within the United States, is as follows: *

Ft. above Sea.

Interior States
- New Mexico.............. 5,660
- Arizona 4,300
- Nevada................... 5,600
- Utah 6,100

Western border State—California........... 2,800
Eastern border State—Texas............... 1,850
Mean height of the six States 4,385

From these Tables of Elevations it appears that

---

* Gannett, pp. 160-162.

half of the Southwest, lying within the United States, is, like old Mexico, highly elevated, and the most so in the interior. Contrasted with the United States, the great interior of New Spain is convex, while the great interior, or Mississipi Valley of the United States is concave. In other words, one is chiefly table-lands, and the other chiefly valley.

ITS REMARKABLE SITUATION.

No country in the whole world is so favored in its situation between oceans and nations, and on the highway of the world's commerce, as is New Spain. It has a coast-line of 7,513 miles.

It lies between the warm streams of the North Atlantic and North Pacific. That portion of the equatorial current which enters the Gulf of Mexico south of the West Indies, encircles the larger portion of the gulf, and flows out north of the West Indies to help form the gulf or warm stream of the North Atlantic, has a positive effect upon the whole eastern coast of New Spain. One part of the Kurosiwo, or warm stream of the North Pacific, flows down along the western coast of New Spain, bringing its characteristic climatic influences and blessings.*

---

* "Gateways to the Pole," by Silas Bent, St. Louis, 1872.

The oceans nearly meet at Tehuantepec, which constitutes the southern extremity of New Spain; and should the long talked-of canal be constructed, opening a new and short route between the ports of the Atlantic and Pacific, there would be a remarkable saving of distance in the voyage from New York to San Francisco, viz.:

Statute Miles.

New York to San Francisco (via Cape Horn).................................	16,360
New York to San Francisco (via Tehuantepec)..................................	4,741
Saving of distance (via Tehuantepec)..	11,619

Vessels sailing from New York to China and Japan usually go by way of Cape of Good Hope instead of Cape Horn. Could they cross New Spain by means of a ship canal the saving of distance would be very great, as the following table of distances shows:

	Via Cape of Good Hope.	Via Tehuantepec.	Saving of Distance.
	(Naut. Miles.)	(Naut. Miles.)	(Naut. Miles.)
New York to Japan (Yokohama).	15,150	9,435	5,715
" China (Hong Kong)	14,015	10,755	3,260

New Spain, in competition with England for the

trade of China and Japan, has a decided advantage in situation, notwithstanding England has shortened her route by use of the Suez Canal. Taking, for the comparison, San Diego, which is the central one of the great harbors of New Spain, and Liverpool, which is the leading harbor of England, and giving England the benefit of the shortest possible route, which is *via* Suez, the result is as follows : *

	Naut. Miles.
Liverpool to China (Hong Kong)	9,568
San Diego " "	6,861
Difference in favor of San Diego	2,707
Liverpool to Japan (Yokohama)	11,403
San Diego " "	5,139
Difference in favor of San Diego	6,264

But Benton's historical exclamation, "There is the East! there is India!" in his great speech in favor of a Pacific Railway at the National Convention in St. Louis, in 1849, has lost some of its commercial significance since the Southwest has developed such marvelous riches. We have a more

---

* These tables of distances are compiled from statistics prepared at the Hydrographic Bureau, and from a publication by H. Stuckle on "Inter-oceanic Canals and Distances."

magnificent country than India at our own door, and instead of dwelling upon the international advantages of New Spain, we will consider its intrinsic wealth.

CHAPTER II.

ITS WEALTH IN SILVER AND GOLD.

THE TREASURES OF THE TOLTECS AND AZTECS.

In its grand westward course the star of empire has reached the Pacific coast, and for some time has been glowing with unusual splendor amidst the wonderful riches of California and Nevada. Its circle was complete when it reached the ocean, opposite Asia, the starting-point of civilization and commerce. It must now stand still, again encircle the globe, or deflect its course to a position nearer the center of the great Southwest. What attractive forces does New Spain possess? And do we find abundant allurements in silver and gold? The record of the mines is very incomplete until the thirst for gold had incited Cortez's army to almost superhuman achievements in subjecting the Aztecs to the crown of Spain.

But here and there we find detached allusions to the treasures of the native races, their working of the mines, and their unrivaled skill as goldsmiths.

Indeed so great was their skill as artists in the working of precious metals, that the proud and usually illiberal conquerors were compelled to admit the Aztec superiority in this respect.* How great were their products of silver and gold from the seventh century, the beginning of their authentic history, down to 1521, a period of about nine hundred years, we can only conjecture. But history has preserved sufficient data about the splendors of that early civilization to prove that the sum total of products of the mines must have been exceedingly large.

New Spain, or such portions of it as were occupied by the civilized nations of the native races, was, from about 600 A. D. to the Spanish invasion, successively ruled by the Toltecs, the Chichimecs, and the Aztecs,† the Toltec supremacy being the longest. Those nations may have preserved records of the workings of the mines, for they were well advanced in learning, as well as wealth and luxuries. The Spanish found, at the Aztec capital, a large collection of histories and public documents, which they consigned to the flames; and, for aught we know, those records may have contained much information in regard to the precious metals.

---

* " History of the Conquest of Mexico," by W. H. Prescott, i. 140.
† See " Native Races of Pacific States," by H. H. Bancroft, v. 158.

Prescott, the historian, says of the Toltecs, they "were the true fountains of the civilization which distinguished this part of the continent in later times."* Humboldt says of the tenth century, under Toltec rule, that "Mexico was in a more advanced state of civilization than Denmark, Sweden, and Russia."† The historian of the "Native Races of the Pacific States" testifies to the same effect as follows: "If the ancient traditions may be believed, the Toltec monarchs built as magnificent palaces as their Aztec successors. The sacred palace of that mysterious Toltec priest-king, Quetzalcoatl, had four principal halls facing the four cardinal points. That on the east was called the Hall of Gold, because its halls were ornamented with plates of that metal delicately chased and finished; * * * the hall facing the south was decorated with plates of silver, and with brilliant-colored sea-shells which were fitted together with great skill."‡ The Italian historian of Mexico says: "The Toltecs were the most celebrated people of Anahuac for their superior civilization and skill in the arts; whence, in after ages, it has been common to distinguish the most remarkable artists, in an honorable manner, by the appellation

---

* Prescott's "Conquest of Mexico," i. 12.
† Humboldt's "Researches in America," p. 83.
‡ Bancroft's "Native Races," ii. 173.

of Toltecas. * * * They had the art of casting gold and silver, and melting them in whatever forms they pleased." * More testimony might be given showing the Toltecs were very proficient in the arts, and had advanced to a high degree of civilization, and splendor. But it is too general in its nature to assist in forming an estimate of their supply of the precious metals.

The Spanish and other historians have left us fuller accounts of the treasures of the Aztecs. Bernal Diaz, who was one of Cortez's soldiers in the invasion of Mexico, kept memoranda of events, and in after years, when he had returned to Spain, used them as a basis for a history of that remarkable conquest. His writings contain frequent allusions to the presents from the Aztec king. The first mention is of one sent by Montezuma to the Spanish camp, before they had advanced toward the capital, or Tenochtitlon, as it was then called. He says, after describing the speech of the official who brought the presents, " he then brought forth, out of a species of box, a quantity of gold trinkets of beautiful and skillful workmanship." †

Again, he tells of an embassy sent from Montezuma to meet Cortez, who had then started on his march for the capital. The ambassadors were ac-

---

* " History of Mexico," by F. S. Clavigero, i. 114.
† " The Memoirs of the Conquistador Bernal Diaz," i. 88.

companied by an hundred Indian porters well laden with presents of various kinds: " The first was a round plate, about the size of a wagon wheel, representing the sun, the whole of the finest gold, and of the most beautiful workmanship, a most extraordinary work of art, which, according to the account of those who weighed it, was worth above twenty thousand gold pesos. The second was a round plate, even larger than the former, of massive silver, representing the moon, with rays and other figures on it, being of great value. The third was the casque, completely filled with pure grains of gold, as they are found in the mines, worth about three thousand pesos, which was more to us than if it had been ten times the value, as we now knew for certain there were rich gold mines in the country. Among other things there were also thirty golden ducks, exactly resembling the living bird, and of splendid workmanship; further figures resembling lions, tigers, dogs, and apes; likewise ten chains, with lockets, all of gold, and of the most costly workmanship." *

Diaz tells of another embassy, with a message from Montezuma to Cortez, while at the city of Tlascalla, which " was accompanied by a valuable present in gold trinkets, of various workmanship, worth about one thousand pesos." † Another, which

---

* Idem, i. 90 and 91. † Idem, p. 170.

met Cortez at some place on the march toward Mexico, with "presents consisting of gold trinkets, of various workmanship, worth about ten thousand pesos."* He tells of another embassy from Montezuma which was accompanied, as usual, with "a present in gold trinkets, of various workmanship, worth altogether above two thousand pesos."† Again, of an embassy which brought "presents in gold and cotton stuffs." ‡

All of these presents, sent to Cortez, were before his first visit to the capital and Montezuma's palace. In Diaz's description of the first peaceful entry of the Spanish troops, and the very hospitable reception by the Aztec king, he says that, when Montezuma conducted Cortez to a room in the palace, he " hung about his neck a chaste necklace of gold, most curiously worked with figures all representing crabs." §

But the bounteous hospitality shown to the Spaniards did not satisfy their greed for gold, and soon Montezuma was detained by them as a prisoner. They used the arts of diplomacy to accomplish their ends, and Cortez succeeded in persuading Montezuma to collect large quantities of treasures to send to the king of Spain. It seems that prior to this event the Spanish, while in possession of

---

* Idem, p. 190.   † Idem, p. 210.
‡ Idem, p. 216.   § Idem, p. 223.

the Aztec palace, had discovered a secret chamber or storehouse of treasures in gold and silver. This discovery they withheld from Montezuma. Diaz tells how Montezuma sent to the officials of the various provinces of his empire for gold to help fill out the proposed present; how he added to the collection the treasures of the secret chamber; that "when the articles were set apart in three heaps and weighed, the silver and other precious things was found to be worth above 600,000 pesos; in this are not included the gold plates, bars and gold-dust contributed by the other provinces." * The reader will observe that values are given for only a small portion of these presents, but the total of those which have values attached is 636,000 pesos, or $7,422,120.† How much that would be increased if the value of the other treasures was stated is a matter for conjecture.

All of these acquisitions of treasure by the Spaniards were prior to the sanguinary battles which led to the downfall of the Aztec empire. Soon after the last-mentioned present, they became alarmed at the conduct of the natives, and made a precipitous retreat from the city. While fleeing across the causeway over the lake, they were fiercely at-

---

* Idem, p. 277-279.

† The value of *pesos* is, according to Prescott, eleven dollars and sixty seven cents. He says that Diaz always means *pesos de oro*, which is different from *pesos*, or the Spanish dollar.—PRESCOTT, i. 320, 321.

tacked, and, according to Prescott, lost in the lake "chests of solid ingots" of their spoils.* After describing their return and attack upon the city, and its final capture, Prescott tells how the Spanish were bitterly disappointed in the amount of booty found; how they believed the Aztecs had buried or hidden the larger portion of the valuables; how they tortured Guatomozin, one of the Aztec officials, to tell where the treasure was secreted, and how he replied "that much gold had been thrown into the water;" † how they searched in a pond in the garden of this prince, and found "a sun, as it is called, probably one of the Aztec calendar wheels, made of pure gold of great size and thickness." ‡ Prescott evidently inclines to the opinion that the Spanish were right in their suspicions, and that the Aztecs had delighted in defeating the greed of the conquerors by secreting much treasure.

THE WORKING OF THE MINES BY THE TOLTECS AND AZTECS.

But where did this great mass of gold and silver come from? That question excited the curiosity of the Spaniards, and they took early steps to trace the localities of the mines. Diaz says that soon after Montezuma was made a prisoner, Cortez asked him where the mines were, and on the strength of

---

* Prescott, ii. 366.   † Prescott, iii. 234.   ‡ Idem, p. 235.

the information received in reply sent out three expeditions to discover them; that one of the three brought back three hundred pesos of gold-dust, and reported that "the caziques of the province employed numbers of the inhabitants at the rivers to wash gold out of the sand in small troughs." He says of the second expedition, that it did not "return with empty hands;" and of the third, under Pizarro, that it brought back gold-dust of the value of one thousand pesos; that Pizarro reported a visit to the Chinantec caziques, "who ordered a number of the inhabitants to repair to the river, to wash the gold-dust from the sand. The gold-dust here found is of a curly shape, and the inhabitants said the mines where the metal was found in that shape were much more productive, and the metal more solid." *

Prescott says of working of the veins of silver and other metals, "in the solid rock into which they opened extensive galleries," that "the traces of their labors furnished the best indications for the early Spanish miners;" that "gold found on the surface or gleaned from the beds of rivers was cast into bars, or, in the form of dust, made part of the regular tribute of the southern provinces of the empire." †

---

* Diaz's "Memoirs," i. 273-276.
† Prescott's "Conquest," i. 138, 139.

Lastly, Baron Humboldt, who had studied the resources of New Spain more closely than any other writer, said: "Long before the arrival of the Spaniards, the nations of Mexico, as well as those of Peru, were acquainted with the use of several metals. They did not content themselves with those which were found in their native state on the surface of the earth, and particularly in the beds of rivers and the ravines formed by the torrents; they applied themselves to subterraneous operations in the working of veins; they cut galleries and dug pits of communication and ventilation, and they had instruments adapted for cutting the rock."*

Such is the array of testimony of the historians. It proves that the civilized native races worked the mines in an extensive and scientific manner; that they possessed enormous quantities of treasure; and that, as artists in the working of gold and silver they were more skillful than the goldsmiths of Europe. Adding to this evidence the fact that the Aztec nation was very numerous, that their cities were many and large, their architecture costly and magnificent, and their living luxurious, it is apparent that the sum total of their products of silver and gold must have been very large. But it is impossible to affix a definite value. Only by a com-

---

* Humboldt's "New Spain," iii. 109.

parison of their products with those since the conquest can an estimate of the value be obtained, and that must be an unsatisfactory one.

It may not seem unreasonable to suppose that the total products of gold and silver in the Southwest, under the civilization of the native races, for a period of nine hundred years, was equal to one-fifth of the total products during the three hundred and fifty-five years since the conquest.

What, then, have the mines yielded since the Spanish invasion?

PRODUCT OF SILVER AND GOLD OF MEXICO, 1521–1804.*

For the statistics of this period Baron Humboldt is the standard authority, and his estimates have been accepted as correct by nearly every historian and statistician. His great reputation as a scientific man procured for him unusual privileges from

---

* This period is to, but not inclusive of, 1804. Whenever a period is mentioned in this chapter, the estimates are inclusive of the first year, but not inclusive of the last. The reader, if he has occasion to compare any of these estimates with those of the authorities from which they are taken, may occasionally meet with an apparent mistake; but on examination he will find the discrepancy owing to the fact that the figures of the original source are inclusive of the last year. There is such a difference of statisticians in this respect, and so frequent an omission to tell whether the estimates are or are not inclusive of the last year, that great care is necessary in making quotations.

the king of Spain, who allowed him the freedom of the Spanish colonial possessions in America for the purposes of his explorations and report. How well he improved the opportunity is shown by the completeness of the report on the resources of New Spain. In compiling his statistics be made use of the official registry of coinage for the period 1690–1804. But for the period 1521–1690 he based his calculations partly upon official records and partly upon estimates of his own, for the registry was incomplete prior to 1690.

The amount of coinage of gold and silver of New Spain (Mexico and New Spain then being interconvertible terms), as stated by him, is as follows: *

1521–1548................	$40,500,000
1548–1690................	374,000,000
1690–1804................	1,353,452,000
Total coinage...........	$1,767,952,000

To this he adds one-seventh, or, in round numbers, $260,000,000, for that portion of the product of the mines which, for various reasons, failed to pass through the mints, making the total products of gold and silver for the whole period, ending at the beginning of 1804, $2,027,952,000.

---

* Humboldt, iii. 413–420.

PRODUCTS OF SILVER AND GOLD OF MEXICO, 1804–1848.

For the products of silver and gold of Mexico for the period 1804–1848 (this period, also, being prior to the cessions of territory to the United States, and New Spain and Mexico being one and the same territory), the statistics of Danson read before the Statistical Society of London, in 1850, are very elaborate and sufficiently cautious to be inside rather than outside the true amount.

They are so well substantiated by explanations and reasoning that we will adopt them in preference to the estimates of any other authority.* He based his calculations for the period 1804–1847 upon the returns of the British consuls and the work in Spanish of M. St. Clair Duport. For the year 1847 he took an average of the products of the five preceding years. It will be observed that Danson includes the year 1848, and that the following statistics differ because of the omission of that year, and it is better to include 1848 in the next period, as it is the beginning of the yield of gold in California.

The registered product of gold for the period 1804–1848 is $31,038,815. And the registered product of silver is $548,334,598. Danson estimates

---

* Journal of Statistical Society of London, xiv. 26, 27.

the registered product of gold as three-eighths of
the whole product, and the registered product of
silver as four-fifths of the whole product. We have,
then, as the total product of gold of New Spain for
the period 1804–1848, $82,770,173; the total pro-
duct of silver, $685,418,247; and the total product
of both metals, $768,188,420.

PRODUCT OF SILVER AND GOLD OF MEXICO, 1848–1876.

For this period Mexico and New Spain are not
identical, for New Spain was divided at the close
of the Mexican war. We will, then, hereafter consider separately the products of Mexico and the
other divisions of New Spain.

The Commissioner of the General Land Office,
in his annual report for 1867, made a special and
very elaborately prepared report on the products of
the precious metals. He estimates the products of
Mexico to the beginning of 1868 as follows: *

	Gold.	Silver.	Both Metals.
1848–1868,	$50,000,000	$420,000,000	$470,000,000

The report estimates the annual product (the
time of writing being 1867) as $26,000,000 in silver
and $3,000,000 in gold. Phillips, an English au-
thority whose estimates are much quoted, said of

---

* Report of Commissioner of General Land Office for 1867, p. 187.

Mexico in 1867: " Since 1850, however, the mines of Mexico have regained their ancient prosperity, and their present annual produce cannot be much less than $26,000,000 in silver and $3,200,000 in gold." *

The United States Consul-General at Mexico, in his report to the State Department, estimates the products of Mexico, for 1875, as $75,000 in gold, and $27,000,000 in silver.

For the eight years 1868 to 1876, we will adopt the estimate of the annual product, as given by the Commissioner of the General Land Office,† which makes the silver product, $208,000,000, and the gold product, $24,000,000.

The total product of both metals in Mexico is, then, as follows:

1848–1876................. $702,000,000

PRODUCT OF SILVER AND GOLD OF CALIFORNIA, 1848–1876.

For the products of the precious metals of this State and other States in the cession from Mexico, we have as authority the various reports of the United States Commissioner of Mining Statistics

---

* " The Mining and Metallurgy of Gold and Silver," by J. A. Phillips, p. 269–270.

† See Report for 1867, p. 187.

except for the year 1876. Unfortunately the report for that year was left unprovided for by Congress.

The reports are ten in number, and for the years 1866 to 1875, inclusive. The second report by J. Ross Browne, the first Commissioner, gives an estimate of the product from the first discovery of gold in 1848 to the beginning of 1868.* Adopting that estimate and the annual estimates thereafter to 1876, we have, as the total product of gold and silver, the following:

1848–1868	$900,000,000
1868	22,000,000
1869	22,500,000
1870	25,000,000
1871	20,000,000
1872	19,049,098
1873	18,025,722
1874	20,300,531
1875	17,753,151
Total 1848–1876	$1,064,628,502

It will be observed that according to the above table the average annual yield of the California mines, during the first twenty years after the commencement of mining operations, was $45,000,000, or more than double what it has been since. The largest product was in 1853, when it reached

---
* See Report for 1867, p. 6

$65,000,000.* The average annual product for the whole period of twenty-eight years is $38,022,446.

PRODUCT OF SILVER AND GOLD OF NEVADA, 1848–1876.

The mines of Nevada were not worked until 1859, when silver was first discovered. The products of the precious metals, as estimated in the various official reports of the United States Commissioner of Mining Statistics, down to the beginning of 1876, are:

1848–1868	$90,000,000
1868	14,000,000
1869	14,000,000
1870	16,000,000
1871	22,500,000
1872	25,548,801
1873	35,254,507
1874	35,452,233
1875	40,478,369
Total	$293,233,910

The average annual product of this Territory, from the discovery of silver in 1859 to the beginning of 1876, a period of seventeen years, was $17,249,053.

---

* Raymond's estimate in vol. iii. Transactions of the American Institute of Mining Engineers, p. 202.

PRODUCT OF SILVER AND GOLD OF ARIZONA, 1848–1876.

Arizona was a portion of the Territory of New Mexico until 1863, when it was organized as a separate Territory. The Government Commissioner of Mining Statistics estimates the combined products of New Mexico and Arizona, from 1848 to 1868, as $5,000,000.* It is probably nearly correct to consider New Mexico and Arizona as equal in their products for that period. Beginning with 1868, the Commissioner gives the separate products down to 1876:

1848–1868	$2,500,000
1868	500,000
1869	1,000,000
1870	800,000
1871	800,000
1872	625,000
1873	500,000
1874	487,000
1875	750,000
Total, 1848–1876	$7,962,000

---

* See Commissioner's Report for 1867, p. 6.

PRODUCT OF SILVER AND GOLD OF NEW MEXICO, 1848-1876.

The mines of New Mexico were worked for many years prior to 1848, but probably in a small manner. Blake says: "The gold field of New Mexico has been known and worked since 1828. The portion so known is confined to the Placer or Gold Mountains, about twenty miles from Santa Fé, towards Albuquerque. The yield of gold has been chiefly from placers, and was estimated by Wislizenus, in 1847, to vary from $30,000 to $250,000 a year, but it soon after diminished, until it became comparatively insignificant."* It is evident they were worked at a much earlier period, and possibly by the native races before the Spanish conquest of New Mexico. Gregg, who was for several years a Santa Fé trader, and was familiar with the Territory of New Mexico, says: "In every quarter of the Territory there are still to be seen vestiges of ancient excavations, and in some places ruins of considerable towns, evidently reared for mining purposes."†

But whatever New Mexico may have yielded in precious metals prior to 1848 is immaterial here, for until then it belonged to Old Mexico, and its

---

* "The Production of the Precious Metals," by W. P. Blake, pp. 43 and 44.

† "Commerce of the Prairies," by Josiah Gregg, i. 164.

product is included in the estimate of that republic on a prior page.

Estimating the product of New Mexico, in the same way we did that of Arizona, the following result is reached as the total of silver and gold:

1848–1868	$2,500,000
1868	250,000
1869	500,000
1870	500,000
1871	500,000
1872	500,000
1873	500,000
1874	500,000
1875	325,000
Total, 1848–1876	$6,075,000

PRODUCT OF SILVER AND GOLD OF UTAH, 1848–1876.

The mines of Utah were not worked in any extensive manner until 1868, although silver was discovered in 1863.* Taking the products of this Territory from the annual reports of the Commissioner of Mining Statistics for the period 1870 to 1876, and prior to that period Prof. Raymond's estimate, as given elsewhere,† we have a total product of silver and gold as follows:

---

* Paper on Utah in American Cyclopædia.   † Idem.

ITS WEALTH IN SILVER AND GOLD.

1868–1869	$600,000
1870	1,300,000
1871	2,300,000
1872	2,445,284
1873	3,778,200
1874	3,911,601
1875	3,137,688
Total, 1848–1876	$17,472,773

PRODUCT OF SILVER AND GOLD OF SOUTHERN AND WESTERN COLORADO FROM 1848–1876.

The product of the whole State, calculated in the same manner as the above products of the Territories, from 1848 to 1876, was $59,695,708.

But it is only Southern and Western Colorado which come within the limits of New Spain, and consequently it is only the products of those portions of the State which are of importance for the purposes of this work.

The larger portion of Grand County, the western half of Summit, most of Lake, the Ute Indian Reservation, all of Saguache, La Plata, Hinsdale, Conejo, Rio Grande, Costilla, Las Animas, Huerfana, the southern half of Fremont, and Pueblo, and the southern third of Bent counties come within the limits of New Spain. According to the report for 1874 of the United States Commissioner of Mining Statistics, the product of precious metal of Colorado, by counties, was as follows :

Clear Creek County		$2,203,947
Gilpin	"	1,631,863
Park	"	596,392
Boulder	"	539,870
Lake	"	223,503
Summit	"	126,188
Southern counties		40,620
Total		$5,362,383

It appears from the above that the Spanish portion of Colorado has, in the past, yielded very little of the annual products of silver and gold. But it is possible that in the future it will furnish the greater portion of the precious metals, for the wonderfully rich mines of the San Juan region in the southwestern portion of the State are about receiving a suitable development.*

TOTAL PRODUCT OF SILVER AND GOLD OF THE SOUTHWEST OF NEW SPAIN—1521–1876.

The above estimates of the products of New Spain, prior to its division of territory in 1848, and of its various divisions since 1848, make the following sum total of products of silver and gold:

---

* United States Commissioner's Report for 1874, p. 358.

ITS WEALTH IN SILVER AND GOLD.

Mexico, 1521–1804	$2,027,952,000
" 1804–1848	768,188,420
" 1848–1876	702,000,000
California, 1848–1876	1,064,628,502
Nevada, 1848–1876	293,233,910
Arizona, 1848–1876	7,962,000
New Mexico, 1848–1876	6,075,000
Utah, 1848–1876	17,472,773
Total of New Spain, 1521–1876,	$4,887,512,605

To the above is to be added the product of silver and gold in the Southwest during the previous nine hundred years of Toltec and Aztec civilization, wealth, and luxury. If the reader thinks the total of that product is equal to one fifth the amount produced during the three hundred and twenty-five years since the conquest of Mexico in 1521, he will have to add about one thousand millions more.

PROGRESS OF MINING IN THE SOUTHWEST.

The amount of *coinage* for different periods, although a little less than the amount of *products* of silver and gold, may serve as well to indicate the progress of the mining industry of the Southwest.

The registered coinage of silver and gold of New Spain, as given by Humboldt, for the period 1521 to 1800, by Ward for the period 1800 to 1825, and by Blake for the period 1825 to 1848, is as follows:*

Years.	Amount of Coinage.	Average Annual Coinage.
1521–1548	$40,500,000	$1,500,000
1548–1690	374,000,000	2,647,887
1690–1700	43,871,335	4,387,133
1700–1710	51,731,034	5,173,103
1710–1720	65,747,027	6,574,702
1720–1730	84,153,223	8,415,322
1730–1740	90,529,730	9,052,973
1740–1750	111,855,040	11,185,504
1750–1760	125,750,094	12,575,009
1760–1770	112,828,860	11,282,886
1770–1780	165,181,729	16,518,172
1780–1790	193,504,554	19,350,455
1790–1800	231,080,214	23,108,021
1800–1810	226,285,711	22,628,571
1810–1825	124,560,386	8,304,025
1825–1848	284,499,853	12,369,558

It will be observed that from the conquest in the year 1521, down to 1810, when the native Mexican priest, Hidalgo, attempted a revolution against the merciless rule of the Spanish, the development of the mines was a steady and continuous growth, with but one or two slight exceptions; that during the last decade of the last century, and the first decade of the present century, the mining industry

---

* Humboldt's "New Spain," iii. 294 and 413-420. "Mexico in 1827," by H. G. Ward, l. 286. "Production of the Precious Metals," by Blake, p. 316.

had reached a high degree of development. This was just prior to the attempt in 1810 by Hidalgo and others to establish the independence of Mexico.

Ward attributes the steady increase of the product of the mines, up to 1810, to the influence of the liberal laws and regulations, in regard to mining, prescribed by the Spanish authorities. But mark the falling-off for the fifteen years following this period, including the attempted revolution by Hidalgo, and the successful revolution of 1821, under the lead of Iturbide, also a native Mexican.

Ward says of this period: "After the great convulsions of 1810, 1811, and 1812, nothing remained to denote, amidst the general wreck, the epoch of splendor which had so immediately preceded it."*

The above table of coinage being arranged according to shorter periods than those we have chosen to represent the products, gives a clearer idea of the progress of mining operations in Mexico, prior to 1848, than the average of annual products. But to illustrate the progress of the whole of New Spain, both prior and subsequent to 1848, a statement of the average annual products is the most convenient manner of reaching the result.

Using the totals of products of silver and gold of New Spain, as given in the preceding pages, the average annual products are as follows:

---

* Ward, i. 400.

1521–1804 (283 years).......... $7,165,908
1804–1848 (44 years).......... 17,458,827
1848–1876 (28 years).......... 74,691,863

PRODUCTS OF SILVER AND GOLD OF THE SOUTHWEST COMPARED WITH EACH OTHER.

Humboldt said at the commencement of the present century: "We may reckon that in times of peace, when the want of mercury does not impede the process of amalgamation, the annual produce of New Spain is, in silver, 22,000,000 of piasters; in gold, 1,000,000 of piasters."[*] Danson gives the separate products of New Spain for the period 1492 to 1804[†] as—

Silver. $1,948,952,000
Gold.................... 79,000,000

For the period 1804 to 1848, Danson estimates the separate products of Mexico to be—

In silver.................. $685,418,247
In gold.................... 82,770,173

The estimates of the separate products of gold and silver of Mexico are, for the next period, and as given on previous pages of this chapter, as follows:

---

[*] Humboldt, iii. 147.
[†] Journal of Statistical Society of London, 1851, p. 19.

ITS WEALTH IN SILVER AND GOLD.

1848–1868, silver............ $420,000,000
    gold............ 50,000,000

And for the period

1868–1876, silver............ $208,000,000
    gold............ 24,000,000

The product of the precious metals of California are usually considered, and estimated, as all gold, hence for this State there is no comparison to be made. The gold product, as previously given, is for the period 1848–1876, $1,064,628,502.

Nevada, in marked contrast, is a silver-producing State, but its product is not all silver.* Raymond divides the total product of that State, for the year 1875, as follows : †

Silver.................... $28,332,151
Gold..................... 12,146,218

This division makes the silver product about 70 per cent. of the total product, or, to be exact, $69\frac{99}{100}$ per cent.

The whole product of precious metals of this State, from the first working of the mines to 1874, inclusive, is separated in an estimate given in the

---

* There seems to be a conflict of opinion in regard to the proper division of the product of Nevada. The forthcoming report of the Silver Commission will doubtless review in detail the ratio of silver to gold.

† See Commissioner's Report for 1875, chapter on Nevada.

paper on Nevada, in the American Cyclopædia, which estimate is credited to Professor Raymond. The silver, as there given, is $74\frac{14}{100}$ per cent. of the combined products. As this is a greater percentage of silver than given for the single year 1875, we will divide the product of Nevada for the whole period to 1876 as follows: 74 per cent. silver and 26 per cent. gold. We have as the result:

  Silver....................$216,993,093
  Gold....................... 76,240,817

Relying upon the same authorities for an estimate of the separate products of Utah, for the year 1875, and also for the period prior to that year, commencing with the first development in 1868, we have the following as the result:

  1868–1876, silver............$15,925,485
      gold............. 1,547,292

It is impossible to give a satisfactory division of the products of New Mexico or of Arizona. In fact the authorities widely differ in regard to the amount of the combined products. But the small amounts of the products of those undeveloped Territories since 1848, will not, if inaccurately stated, make any essential difference in the general comparison of silver and gold of the whole of New Spain for the long period 1521 to 1876. New Mexico was formerly considered a gold-producing State, but for the year 1875 the Commissioner of Mining Statistics considers the product nearly all silver. Arizona produces both gold and silver. It may not be far from correct to combine the products of precious metals of the two Territories, and estimate the same as half silver and half gold. We have, then, as the separate products of the two Territories for the period 1848-1876—

Silver........................$7,018,500
Gold......................... 7,018,500

A summary of the above gives as the result of the comparison the following:

		Silver Product.	*Gold Product.*
Mexico	1492-1804	$1,948,952,000	$79,000,000
"	1804-1848	685,418,247	82,770,173
"	1848-1868	420,000,000	50,000,000
"	1868-1876	208,000,000	24,000,000
California	1848-1876	——	1,064,628,502
Nevada	1848-1876	216,993,093	76,240,817
Utah	1848-1876	15,925,485	1,547,292
Ariz. and New Mex.	1848-1876	7,018,500	7,018,500
Total		$3,502,307,325	$1,385,205,284

The totals show that of the precious metals produced by the Southwest, from its first settlement by Cortez, down to the beginning of the year 1876, $71\frac{6}{10}$ *per cent., or nearly three-fourths, was silver.*

PRODUCT OF SILVER AND GOLD OF THE SOUTHWEST COMPARED WITH THAT OF THE WORLD.

Perhaps no more carefully prepared estimate of the world's product of silver and gold can be found than Wilson's estimate, from the discovery of America, in 1492, to the commencement of 1868. Of course it is impossible to give the products of the uncivilized portion of the world. Wilson's estimate includes America, Europe, Asiatic Russia, Australia, New Zealand, and portions of Northern Africa.* The following estimate of the world's product of silver and gold from 1868 to 1876 is from the "Journal des Economistes," quoted in the elaborate Report of the Select Committee of Parliament, in 1876, on the depreciation of silver.† The amount of silver and gold produced in the world since the discovery of America is as follows:

1492–1868	$11,766,825,889
1868–1876	1,345,000,000
Total	$13,111,825,889

We have taken the product of the world from 1492, as nearly all statistics of the world's products

---

* Report of Commissioner of General Land Office for 1867, p. 213.

† Report from the Select Committee on Depreciation of Silver, p. 140 of Appendix.

of precious metals are arranged according to certain periods, one of which invariably begins with the discovery of America. But New Spain's statistics begin with 1521, so in the following comparison the world has the advantage by twenty-nine years. The comparison shows that New Spain produced thirty-seven per cent., or considerably over one-third of the silver and gold of the whole world.

PRODUCT OF SILVER AND GOLD OF MEXICO SINCE 1848, COMPARED WITH THAT OF THE TERRITORY CEDED BY HER TO THE UNITED STATES.

Referring to the statistics on previous pages, we find the total product of silver and gold of Mexico, from 1848 to 1876, to be $702,000,000, and the total product of the territory ceded by her to the United States, in 1848 and 1853, was, for the same period, $1,389,372,185. In other words, the territory ceded by Mexico has, since 1848, yielded twice as much silver and gold as the territory she retained.

PRODUCT, SINCE 1848, OF SILVER AND GOLD OF THE TERRITORY ACQUIRED FROM MEXICO, COMPARED WITH THAT OF THE REST OF THE UNITED STATES.

Referring again to the statistics above given on previous pages, we find the total product of silver and gold, from 1848 to 1876, of the various States and Territories of the acquisitions from Mexico in 1848 and 1853, was $1,389,372,185. The product of the whole United States, according to Raymond, is, from 1848 to 1876, $1,574,045,802.* Deducting from that total the amount of the product of the territory acquired from Mexico, and there is left, as the product of the rest of the United States, $184,673,617. In other words, over seven-eighths of the silver and gold of the whole United States from 1848 to 1876 was produced by the territory acquired from Mexico. Who will say that our investment was not a profitable one?

SILVER PRODUCT OF THE SOUTHWEST, OR NEW SPAIN, COMPARED WITH THAT OF THE WHOLE WORLD.

Baron Humboldt wrote, about the beginning of the present century, "The two millions and a half of marcs of silver annually exported from Vera Cruz *are equal to two-thirds of the silver annually extracted from the whole globe.*" †

But what portion of the world's product has the Southwest furnished since the discovery of America, and why is the Southwest entitled to be called the silver country?

---

* See Raymond's Annual Report, viii. 544, and also Annual Reports for years 1874, 1865.

† Humboldt's "New Spain," iii. 146.

ITS WEALTH IN SILVER AND GOLD. 61

The following estimates of the world's yield of silver, from 1492 to 1868, are from the statistics of Wilson; and by the world is meant America, Europe, Asiatic Russia, Australia, New Zealand, and portions of Northern Africa, those being the only portions whose products can be ascertained.*
The estimate of the world's silver, from 1868 to 1876, is that given by the United States Bureau of Statistics, as published in the British report on the depreciation of silver.†

The statistics of the silver of New Spain are compiled from the estimates and percentages on the preceding pages of this chapter.

Years.	Silver Product of the World.	Silver Product of New Spain.
1492–1804	$4,455,130,000	$1,948,952,000
1804–1848	1,223,781,674	685,418,247
1848–1868	971,060,000	489,100,000
1868–1876	582,100,000	378,837,078
Total, 1492–1876	$7,232,071,674	$3,502,307,325

It will be observed that in the above table the product of New Spain is given commencing with 1492, whereas the tables on previous pages give the product of New Spain as commencing in 1521. But the mines of New Spain were not worked by the Spanish until the conquest in 1521, hence it is

---

* Report of Commissioner of General Land Office for 1867, p. 213.
† See Appendix to that Report, p. 140.

fair to call this the total product from the date of the discovery of America; and as all estimates of the world's products are for certain periods, one of which always commences with 1492, it is impossible to arrange the comparison in any other way.

Still more striking is the comparison of the silver products of the world and New Spain for the year 1875, or the last year of the above table. The British report on the "Depreciation of Silver" gives, in the appendix, three different estimates, each from a different source, of the world's product of silver for 1875. One, in a paper submitted by Sir Hector Hay, is £16,100,000 sterling, or $77,924,000;* a second, from the Bureau of Statistics of the United States, is $77,700,000;† and a third, taken from the "Journal des Economistes," is $62,000,000.‡ The silver product of Mexico, for 1875, according to the United States Consul-General at the city of Mexico, "may safely be estimated at $27,000,000."§ Raymond estimates the silver of Nevada, for 1875, as we have already stated on a previous page, to be $28,332,151; and he estimates the silver of Utah, for 1875, to be

---

* Report on the Depreciation of Silver, Appendix, p. 25.
† Idem, p. 146.
‡ Idem, p. 140.
§ "Commercial Relations of United States with Foreign Countries for 1875," p. 1120.

$2,955,922.* Raymond estimates the silver product of New Mexico, for 1875, to be $225,000.† Calling the silver product of Arizona, for 1875, $375,000, which is one-half of its total product of silver and gold, and combining the above products, we have the total silver product of New Spain for 1875. Selecting the middle one of the above estimates of the world's product, which is that of the Bureau of Statistics, and comparing it with that of New Spain, we have the following result as the silver product for 1875:

> The World.................. $77,700,000
> New Spain.................. 58,888,073

The above comparisons show that the Southwest, from the conquest in 1521 to 1804, yielded forty-three per cent. of the silver product of the whole world; ‡ from 1804 to 1848, fifty-six per cent. of the silver product of the world; from 1848 to 1868, fifty per cent. of the silver product of the world; from 1868 to 1875, sixty-five per cent. of the silver product of the world; and during the year 1875, seventy-five per cent. of the silver product of the world.

---

* See Report of Mining Commissioner for 1875, chapter on Utah.

† Idem, chapter on New Mexico.

‡ The percentage of New Spain would be slightly increased for this period if we could compare it with the world from 1521, instead of giving the world the advantage by twenty-nine years by commencing at 1492.

When the advance of railways makes possible a development of the silver mines of Arizona, New Mexico, and the Northern States of Old Mexico, it is fair to presume the silver product of the Southwest will compare still more favorably with that of the world.

MINERAL WEALTH OF THE BORDER STATES.

There is an abundance of testimony to prove that the richest mines of the republic of Mexico are in the Northern States near the border; and the testimony is equally abundant showing that the portion of New Spain lying within the United States, and just north of the Mexican border, ranks among the richest in silver and gold.

Ward's official report to the British Government, made after several years' residence in Mexico as His Majesty's *Chargé d'Affaires*, is, next to Humboldt's work, the most thorough and comprehensive review of the resources of New Spain, which has ever been published. It says of the States south of the border line:

"The States of Durango, Sonora, Chihuahua, and Sinaloa, contain an infinity of mines hitherto but little known, but holding out, wherever they have been tried, a promise of riches superior to anything that Mexico has yet produced." *

---

* Ward's "Mexico in 1827," i. 452.

Of the mines north of the border, he said:

"I see enough in these records of Arizona to warrant the supposition (confirmed as it is by the facts and appearances mentioned in the preceding pages) that the hitherto unexplored regions in the North of Mexico contain mineral treasures which, as discoveries proceed, are likely to make the future produce of the country infinitely exceed the amount that has been hitherto drawn from the comparatively poorer districts of the South."*

The report of the Mexican Committee on Mining Taxes, made in 1868, says:

"The mineral wealth of the States of Durango, Sonora, and Chihuahua is greater than all the rest of our territory, from certain indications: and it will be developed as soon as settlers are protected from the scalping-knives of the savages." †

Another standard authority says of Sinaloa:

"The State of Sinaloa is said to be literally covered with silver mines." * * * "Scientific explorers, who visited the Sinaloa mines in 1872, reported that those on the Pacific slopes would be the great source of supply of silver for the next century." ‡

---

* Idem, p. 460.
† "Production of the Precious Metals," by Blake, p. 320.
‡ Paper on Mexico, in American Cyclopædia.

Dr. Wislizenus, in his work on Northern Mexico, testifies that "the silver mines of the State of Chihuahua, though worked for centuries, seem to be inexhaustible. The discovery of new mines is but a common occurrence, and, attracted by them, the mining population moves generally from one place to another without exhausting the old ones." * * * "New Mexico seems to be as rich in gold ore as Chihuahua is in silver; but yet less capital and greater insecurity have prevented their being worked to a large extent."*

J. Ross Browne, who was the first United States Commissioner of Mining Statistics, reported in 1868, in regard to the States immediately south of the Pacific border line, as follows:

"Durango is very rich in silver, but its wealth was not known until just before the revolution, and there has been comparatively little exploration since. This State, like Sonora and Chihuahua, has suffered severely from Apache incursions. The city of Durango, one hundred and ninety-five miles northwest of Zacatecas, had only eight thousand inhabitants in 1783; but in that year Zambrano, the great miner of that region, discovered the mines of Guarisamey, and Durango soon trebled its population. In twenty-four years he extracted $30,000,000 from his claims; and a multitude of mines

---

* Dr. Wislizenus's "Tour of Northern Mexico," p. 83.

were opened, so that the average yield of the State was estimated to be $5,000,000." *

Some very valuable testimony in regard to the mineral wealth of Santa Eulalia, in the State of Chihuahua, is to be found in the paper read before the Royal Geographical Society of London, in 1859, by Charles Sevin, F.R.G.S., who had visited Mexico to see "how far the mineral wealth of these regions can be worked to advantage with English capital." He says: "In a space of two square leagues all the mountains of Santa Eulalia contain silver; more than two hundred mines have been worked in these confines, and upwards of fifty of them have been sunk to a depth of two hundred yards. Some of these are so extensive that one whole day will not suffice to see the different parts of one alone. With regard to the immense amount of silver extracted from the mines of Santa Eulalia, the following statements will be found interesting. At the most flourishing time a contribution was raised of two grains of silver from every marc extracted, for the purpose of building two churches; one at the city of Chihuahua, the other at Santa Eulalia. They were built in a few years. The cost of that of Chihuahua was $600,000, of that of Santa Eulalia $150,000; and a surplus of $150,000 of the money

---

* "Resources of the Pacific States," p. 648.

collected in this manner remained. The result of the contribution therefore amounted to $900,000, which corresponds to an amount of 145,000 marcs of silver, worth at the real value of that metal $145,000,000, extracted from the mines of Santa Eulalia in the course of a few years. It cannot be supposed that the produce of these mines, rich as they were up to the last operations, suddenly stopped by the expulsion of the Spaniards, should have retained the same ratio at all periods. However, the whole amount of silver which they have yielded, though it is to be divided over a number of about one hundred and thirty years, will be found very great. In the year 1833, a census of this whole amount was made, and it was found to have been 43,000,000 marcs of silver, or $430,000,000."[*]

Wilson, the historian of Mexico, in one of his three works on Mexico, says: " We have the following record in evidence of the masses of silver extracted at Arazuma. Don Domingo Asmendi paid duties on a piece of virgin silver which weighed 275 lbs. The king's attorney (fiscal) brought suit for the duties on several other pieces, which together weighed 4,033 lbs. Also for the recovery, as a curiosity, and therefore the property of the king, of a certain piece of silver of the weight

---

[*] Journal of Royal Geographical Society for 1860, p. 33.

of 2,700 lbs. This is probably the largest piece of pure silver ever found in the world."*

Arazuma, above alluded to, is in the present Territory of Arizona, and probably in the southern portion, which was part of the Gadsden purchase of 1853.

Ward, the British minister to Mexico, says in his report that he saw the correspondence in regard to those masses of virgin silver, that he obtained a certified copy of the decree, and that its authenticity was unquestionable. He does not accept the whole of the facts recorded as correct. Nevertheless, the record satisfied him that the silver mines of Arizona were richer than those farther south.†

Baron Humboldt says that native silver "has been found in considerable masses, sometimes weighing more than two hundred kilogrammes,‡ in the seams of Batopilas, in New Biscay."§

New Biscay was the same as the former intendancy of Durango, which embraced what are now the border States of Durango and Chihuahua. Batopilas is in Chihuahua.∥

A recent authority on Arizona gives the follow-

---

* " Mexico and Its Religion," by R. A. Wilson, p. 387.
† Ward's " Mexico in 1827," ii. 137.
‡ Four hundred and forty-four lbs. (avoirdupois).
§ Humboldt's " New Spain," iii. 157.
∥ Idem, ii. 237.

ing significant facts and figures in regard to the great mineral wealth of that territory:

The number of "mines located and recorded in the Territory, which was obtained from the county registers of each county, excepting the County of Mohave, which is given much below the actual number, was, on the first day of October, 1876, as follows:

Yavapai County	7,298
Pima County	975
Maricopa County	200
Yuma County	580
Pinal County	552
Mohave County	2,000
Total	11,605 "*

Prof. Raymond, the United States Commissioner, says, in his official report for 1869, of another border State: "Indications of placer gold are very general all over New Mexico; and I believe that with the introduction of hydraulics this interest will become a very prominent one in the future." * * * "Whenever railroads shall traverse this country its mines will be of great value, as they will possess then every facility for successful working."†

---

* " Arizona as It Is; or, The Coming Country," by H. C. Hodge, p. 135.

† See Report for 1869, pp. 408 and 414.

Such is the testimony of the leading writers on the wealth of the border States. We might add almost a volume more to the same effect. But enough has been cited on this point to satisfy the most skeptical, and we will now consider why these remarkable mines are not adding their stores of wealth to the world's supply of precious metals.

PRESENT CONDITION AND WANTS OF THE MINING INDUSTRY.

Those portions of New Spain, such as California and Nevada, which have been so fortunate as to receive a thrifty American civilization, the aid of railways, and a partial development of their resources, are adding each year large contributions to the world's supply of silver and gold, and are furnishing work and good pay to the laboring classes. Old Mexico, another portion of New Spain, suffers for want of better government and a better civilization. Nevertheless, the interior of that republic is producing each year large sums of silver. The annual yield of Mexico, as a whole, is now nearly as large as during the best days of Spanish rule; but still it is not half what it should be. It is the centre of New Spain, or the rich border States, where the mining industry is prostrate. Anarchy, Indian raids, and lack of railroads south of the line, and Apache raids and lack of transportation north of the line, have well-nigh ruined this magnificent border country. Its development has never recovered from the effects of the check it received at the time Mexico entered into the struggle to throw off Spanish authority in 1810.

The contrast between the former flourishing condition of the Santa Eulalia mines, which are above described, and their present prostration is well described by Sevin, who said in 1859: "Since the interruption of the regular mining operations in 1833, the inhabitants of Santa Eulalia have nevertheless almost entirely existed upon the produce of the unscientific and disconnected operations which are carried on in nearly all the abandoned mines of this country. In this manner these mines have continued to support a population of one thousand five hundred souls in this little town, and have contributed also to the maintenance of a surrounding scattered population, which supplies the miners with wood, coal, provisions, etc."* In the palmy days of the mining industry under the Spanish, the city of Chihuahua had a population of over seventy thousand inhabitants. Now it has but twelve thousand.†

The United States consul at Guaymas, in a com-

---
* Journal of Royal Geographical Society for 1860, p. 33.
† Paper on Chihuahua in American Cyclopædia.

munication to the State Department in 1873, said of the condition of affairs in Sonora: " The Indian plague of Apache raids from Arizona still continues, and during the first quarter of the year was particularly severe. In that time one hundred and fifty persons—men, women, and children, Mexicans—were killed."* Wilson said about 1851, of this same border State : " The capitalists of Mexico will not invest their means in developing the resources of Sonora, and in consequence the finest country in the world is fast receding to a state of nature." †

Just before the late civil war in the United States a large amount of capital was attracted by the mining industry of Arizona, and an effort was made to develop its great silver mines. Costly machinery was taken over the plains, and operations were fairly under way when the outbreak of the war caused the Government troops to be recalled from the Territory, and the Apache Indians and Mexicans immediately improved the opportunity to make havoc of the costly works at the mines. Soon after this, in the year 1863, J. Ross Browne visited Arizona, and he says of the rich Heintzelman mine which we have described above: " At the time of our

---

* See Report for 1873 on " Commercial Relations of the United States with Foreign Countries," p. 831.
† " Mexico and its Religion," p. 388.

visit it was silent and desolate, a picture of utter abandonment. The adobe houses were fast falling into ruins; the engines were no longer at work; the rich piles of ore lying in front of the shafts had been sacked and robbed by marauding Mexicans; nothing was to be seen but wreck and ruin." *

The disturbed condition of the border States during the past few years is too fresh in the minds of the reader to need recital here. Until anarchy is supplanted by good government no adequate development may be expected. But north of the border, in Arizona and New Mexico, during the past few years, the danger from Apache raids has not been as great as it was during the late civil war. And regardless of the fact that facilities for transportation are very incomplete, some little progress has been made in the mining industry. The report of the Mining Commissioner for 1874 says of Arizona: "From the southern portion of this Territory have come frequent reports during the year just past of the revival of a once flourishing mining industry, which had, however, for years been actually wiped out of existence by the Apache Indians." †

The report of the United States Mining Commissioner for 1875 contains a review of the mining industry of Arizona, which says: " The past year has

---

* " Adventures in the Apache Country," by J. Ross Browne, p. 266.
† See Report for 1874, p. 389.

witnessed an increased attention to mining and the investment of some new capital; but the distances both from the Pacific and the Atlantic States are such, and many of the roads to the mineral districts are so heavy, or rough, that no expeditions and economical movement of ores, machinery, or miners, no working or shipment of low-grade ores, and no influx of capital (even from California) can be looked for, and consequently no extensive or very important operations can be carried on until, at least, a trunk railroad crosses the Territory." *

Regardless of the overwhelming testimony proving the great mineral wealth of Arizona, New Mexico, Chihuahua, Durango, and Sinaloa, and of the fact that there are some indications of a new development north of the border, the late annual reports of the United States Commissioner fail to show very large products in New Mexico and Arizona. The mines are stagnant at a time when the science of mining has become almost perfect, when every facility, in the shape of improved and effective machinery, is awaiting the assistance of capital. There is but one remedy for the present lack of progress, and that is, suitable transportation for troops, for mining machinery, and for the advance of a thrifty civilization.

---

* See Report for 1875, p. 341.

THE FUTURE PRODUCTS OF SILVER AND GOLD OF THE SOUTHWEST.

Great as were the treasures which the Spanish unlocked from the mines, they did little more, say the standard authorities, than work the surface ores. When the mine became too deep and the labor difficult they abandoned it and moved elsewhere, to repeat at some other mine the same superficial process. Still less thorough was the working of the mines by the Mexicans after they declared their independence from Spain. But one portion of New Spain has received the blessings of a progressive civilization, and the wonderful development of the mines of California and Nevada, since they became a part of the United States in 1848, is an indication of what we may expect as the future products of the whole Southwest. California alone, from 1848 to 1876, produced more precious metals than the whole republic of Mexico, or $1,064,628,502 against Mexico's $702,000,000. The wonderful progress of this State with an energetic people is a fair illustration of the possibilities of Mexico with the same aids to advancement. Sevin, who visited Mexico in 1856, and, as we have above stated, reported his observations to the Royal Geographical Society in 1859, said: " It is generally known and admitted that the mineral wealth of the country hitherto explored is but a drop in the ocean compared with the virgin mines which exist in every direction, only wanting capital and enterprise for their development." * Baron Humboldt expressed a similar opinion at the commencement of the present century, and at a time when the annual product of silver and gold of New Spain averaged about $26,959,357. He said: "The opinion that New Spain produces only, perhaps, the third part of the precious metals which it could supply under happier political circumstances, has been long entertained by all the intelligent persons who inhabit the principal districts of mines of that country, and is formally announced in a memoir presented by the deputies of the body of miners to the king in 1774, a production drawn up with great wisdom and knowledge of local circumstances." †

Not only has nature been very liberal in the mineral endowment of New Spain, but she has stored the vast quantities of silver and gold in accessible places. Humboldt says: "A remarkable advantage for the progress of national industry arises from the height at which nature in New Spain has deposited the precious metals. In Peru the most considerable mines, those of Potosi, Pasco, and

---

* Journal of the Royal Geographical Society for 1860, p. 52.
† Humboldt's "New Spain," iii. 334, 335.

Chota, are immensely elevated near the region of perpetual snow." * The table-lands of Mexico, which are the principal depositories of the treasures, possess a mild climate, which does not interfere with agreeable and successful work. One thing, however, is wanting, and that is, development. When the whole of New Spain receives that blessing, we may expect the Southwest will not only continue to surpass the rest of the world combined, but even eclipse its own brilliant record in the production of silver.

* Humboldt, i. 70, 71.

CHAPTER III.

OTHER WEALTH THAN SILVER AND GOLD.

OF one portion of New Spain, Daniel Webster said in the United States Senate in 1850: "I am sure that everybody has become satisfied that although California may have a very great seaboard, and a large city or two, yet that the agricultural products of the whole surface now are not, and never will be, equal to one-half part of those of the State of Illinois; no, nor yet a fourth, or perhaps a tenth part." *

Yet with a partial development of its agriculture the wheat crop of California in 1875 exceeded in value that of Illinois and every other State of the Union; its product of barley was in value four times that of Illinois, and greater than that of every other State; its wool product was in value nearly double that of Illinois, and greater than the yield of every other State except Ohio; its wheat product was more than ten million dollars in excess of

---

* See Speech on Public Lands, etc., of California, in vol. v. of his works, p. 398.

its gold product; and in 1876 its wheat crop was in value over twelve million dollars in excess of the wheat crop of Illinois.

Texas, another portion of New Spain, although comparatively undeveloped, produced in 1875 corn exceeding in value the corn products of all the New England States and New York combined; its wheat crop, in 1876, was worth over five million dollars, and as it has nearly doubled each year since 1874, its value in the future, when Western Texas is developed, will be doubled many times more; its cotton crop, in 1876, was equal to half the amount consumed in the whole United States, and greater in value than the gold product of California.

Those who under-estimate the agricultural capacity of other parts of the Southwest, and who think that silver and gold comprise the sum total of its riches, have only to await the advance of railways, and a suitable development of New and Old Mexico and Arizona for further surprises and statistical proof of their delusion.

Those keen observers of nature—the civilized native races—selected the table-lands of Mexico as their favorite part of North America for founding an empire. They were entirely dependent upon the resources of their own land for the necessities of life, and could not have maintained for several centuries a civilization celebrated for luxury unless the agricultural capacities were equal to their requirements. Nor could the table-lands of New Mexico and Arizona have supported the numerous cities and dense population of their semi-civilized inhabitants unless the products of the soil were great.

But surprising assertions should be sustained by ample authorities, and we will briefly cite some of the facts from the official reports of the United States Commissioner of Agriculture, and other reliable sources.

WHEAT.

In speaking of the table-land in Mexico, extending from Queretaro to Leon, Baron Humboldt said, at the beginning of the present century: " The wheat harvest is thirty-five and forty for one, and several great farms can reckon fifty or sixty to one." * * * "At Cholula, the common harvest is from thirty to forty, but it frequently exceeds from seventy to eighty for one. In the valley of Mexico, the maize yields two hundred, and the wheat eighteen or twenty. I have to observe that the numbers which I here give have all the accuracy which can be desired in so important an object for the knowledge of territorial riches. Being eagerly desirous of knowing the produce of agriculture under the tropics, I procured all the information on the very spots; and I compared together the data which I was furnished by intelligent colonists who inhabited provinces at a distance from one another. I was induced to be so much the more precise in this operation, as, from having been born in a country where grain scarcely produces four or five for one, I was naturally more apt, than another, to be disposed to suspect the exaggerations of agriculturists." * Of another part of Mexico he said: "Near Zelaya, the agriculturists showed me the enormous difference of produce between the lands artificially watered and those which are not. The former, which receive the water of the Rio Grande, distributed by drains into several pools, yield from forty to fifty for one; while the latter, which do not enjoy the benefit of irrigation, only yield fifteen or twenty." † California was then a part of the kingdom of New Spain, and Humboldt includes it in his investigations. He said: "In the northern extremity of the kingdom, on the coast of New California, the produce of wheat is from sixteen to seventeen for one, taking the mean term among the harvests of eighteen villages for two years. I believe that agriculturists will peruse with pleasure the detail of these harvests in a country situated under the same parallel as Algiers, Tunis, and Pal-

---

* Humboldt's "New Spain," ii. 413 and 414.
† Idem, p. 415.

estine, between 32° 39' and 37° 48' of latitude." * After setting forth in detail the wheat-growing capacity of New Spain, he contrasts the statistics with those of other nations as follows: "We shall collect into one table the knowledge which we have acquired as to the mean produce of the cerealia in the two continents. We are not here adducing examples of an extraordinary fertility observable in a small extent of ground." * * * "But in treating of agriculture in general, we speak merely of extensive results, of calculations in which the total harvest of a country is considered as the multiple of the quantity of wheat sown. It will be found that this multiple, which may be considered as one of the first elements of the prosperity of nations, varies in the following manner: five to six grains for one in France, according to Lavoisier and Neckar." * * * "This is also the mean produce in the North of Germany, Poland, and, according to M. Rühs, in Sweden." * * * "Eight to ten grains for one in Hungary, Croatia, and Sclavonia, according to the researches of M. Swartner." * * * "Seventeen grains for one in the northern part of Mexico." * * * "Twenty-four grains for one in the equinoctial region of Mexico." †

---

* Idem, p. 419.   † Idem, pp. 427–428.

He says of the quality: "The Mexican wheat is of the very best quality; and it may be compared with the finest Andalusian grain" * * * "In Mexico the grain is very large, very white, and very nutritive, especially in farms where watering is employed." *

A recent writer on California, since it was separated from Mexico in 1848, says: "I was shown in one field a unique sight, a 'volunteer crop' of wheat which had sprung of itself in a field unbroken and uncultivated from last year's scattered seeds, so rich that it would probably average forty to forty-five bushels to the acre." †

The wheat record of California and Texas, for the past five years, tends to show how reliable and close an observer of the agricultural capacity of the great Southwest was Baron Humboldt. The following tables show the respective rank of the five leading wheat States during each of the past five years. The estimates are compiled from the annual reports of the Commissioner of Agriculture:

1872.

1. Illinois $30,394,530
2. California 28,416,000
3. Ohio 25,848,260

---

* Idem, p. 434.
† "The New West," by C. L. Brace, p. 232.

OTHER WEALTH.

4. Indiana $25,582,920
5. Wisconsin............... 22,976,210

1873.

1. Illinois $31,258,700
2. California 28,385,280
3. Iowa..................... 27,334,000
4. Wisconsin............... 25,532,340
5. Indiana 25,415,040

1874.

1. California............... $28,096,200
2. Ohio 27,032,720
3. Illinois.................. 25,904,920
4. Iowa.................... 22,040,200
5. Indiana 21,931,140

1875.

1. California............... $28,084,000
2. Illinois 24,843,000
3. Minnesota............... 23,392,000
4. Wisconsin 22,932,000
5. Iowa.................... 21,158,000

1876.

1. California............... $34,200,000
2. Ohio 24,795,000
3. Pennsylvania 23,425,000
4. Illinois 21,799,200
5. Indiana................. 20,400,000

The comparison shows that California has been ahead since 1873. No other State of the Union is likely to dispute her leading position unless it be Texas. That State entered the race for wheat supremacy at a late day, but her remarkable capacity for doubling her product each year is not likely to end until she gets near the head.

The following table shows the value of the wheat crop of Texas for each of the past three years: *

```
1874........................ $1,989,900
1875........................  3,187,700
1876........................  5,130,000
```

A commercial writer of the Mississippi Valley, attracted by the remarkable wheat-growing capacity of California, has recently indulged in some speculations in regard to "the shifting of the wheat-producing belt and its commercial significance." After reviewing the great crops of California, the increased yield per acre by the aid of irrigation, the certainty of the crop owing to the absence of rain during harvest-time, the uncertainty of the crop in the Mississippi Valley States because of rain in harvest-time, he draws the following conclusion in regard to certain States, which the reader

---

* These estimates are also from annual reports of the United States Commissioner of Agriculture.

will observe constitute nearly the same country which we have defined to be New Spain, or the Southwest, viz.:

"In view of these things, does it not appear certain, as the State of California settles up, and as railway facilities are extended to Colorado, New Mexico, Old Mexico, Utah, Arizona, Nevada, and Western Texas, the vast belts of country inflicted with 'dry' seasons, but just as capable to produce wheat, by irrigation, as California, does not it appear certain, we again ask, that the surplus wheat of the world will ultimately be grown within this wonderful area?"*

COTTON.

The production of cotton is not a new element of wealth in the Southwest, but is the revival of an industry which flourished under the civilized native races long before America was known to Europeans. All historians agree in regard to the extensive use of cotton by the Aztecs; and what they manufactured they undoubtedly produced, for they had little intercourse with the outside world. The historian of the "Conquest of Mexico," in describing the first presents from Montezuma to Cortez, mentions, as one item, "ten loads of fine cottons."†

---

* Commercial editorial of *St. Louis Republican*, December 4, 1876.
† Prescott's "Conquest of Mexico," i. 302.

Of another embassy, from Montezuma to Cortez, he states that slaves brought as presents " curtains, coverlets, and robes of cotton, fine as silk, of rich and various dyes, interwoven with feather-work that rivaled the delicacy of painting. There were thirty loads of cotton cloth in addition."* Another leading historian of Mexico says: " Cotton was among the indigenous products of Mexico at the time of the conquest; and the early adventurers not only found it to constitute the common vesture of the masses of the people, but also that the most delicate and luxurious articles of dress were made of it. The Aztecs possessed the art of spinning it to an extreme degree of fineness, and of imparting to it the beautiful and brilliant dyes for which they were celebrated; but both those mysteries were entirely lost in the general destruction of aboriginal arts and records by the Spaniards. Notwithstanding the natural anxiety of Spain to furnish her colonists with her manufactures, she could never prevent the people from weaving and wearing this spontaneous product of their soil.† These facts indicate very clearly that Mexico was, before the days of Spanish rule, an extensive producer of cotton. Mexico of the present day produces some cotton, manufactures quite extensively, and imports

---

* Idem. p. 320.
† " Mexico: Aztec, Spanish, and Republican," by B. Mayer, ii. 67.

largely. Mayer says that "in 1843 there were 53 cotton factories in the republic, with a total of 131,280 spindles; and it was estimated that, looking to Mexico alone for the supply, there would be an annual deficiency of a large quantity of the raw material. This calculation, it must be remembered, does not include the consumption of cotton by hand-looms, an immense number of which are in constant use through the republic."* About fifteen years later the investment of capital in buildings and machinery for the manufacture of cotton was, according to Butterfield, $7,372,951.† The annual consumption of cotton by the factories of the three States of Mexico, Puebla, and Queretaro was stated, in the official report of the United States Consul-General for 1874, to be 11,276,000 pounds.‡

But Mexico consumes more cotton than she manufactures or produces, as the record of imports in a subsequent chapter will show. Her largest trade is with England, and the largest item of imports is invariably cotton. Of her total imports, from all countries, for the fiscal year ending June 30th, 1873, which total was, in value, $29,062,406, over one-

---

* Mayer's "Mexico," ii. 68.
† "United States and Mexican Mail Steamship Line," by Carlos Butterfield.
‡ "Annual Report on Commercial Relations," p. 831.

third, or $10,531,970, was in "cotton stuffs." About the adaptability of Mexico to the production of cotton there is no question; but her modern development is delayed. Another portion of New Spain, however, is producing enough cotton to supply the demand of the whole Southwest. Texas, in 1870, was the fifth State of the Union in the number of bales produced, which were 350,628. In 1876 the product was 690,000 bales.* That product placed Texas second in rank among the great cotton-producing States, Mississippi being the only State yielding a larger crop. If we reduce the product to pounds, by calling the average 440 pounds to the bale, the result is 303,600,000 pounds; and estimating the value of each pound at eleven cents (which is the average value of the cotton of the whole United States for 1876, as given by the United States Commissioner of Agriculture,† we have, as the total value of the crop, $33,396,000. In other words, Texas, in 1876, produced cotton nearly double in value the gold product of California in 1875. This cotton crop was grown upon 1,483,500 acres. As Texas possesses in all 175,587,840 acres of land, there seems to be almost no limit to the cotton capacity of this great and fertile State. The cotton consumption of the

---

* See Report of Commissioner of Agriculture for 1876.
† Idem.

whole United States for 1876 is estimated by Edward Atkinson to be 600,000,000 pounds.* Therefore Texas produced last year fully one-half of the amount of cotton consumed in the whole United States.

INDIAN CORN.

The British minister wrote of Mexico, in 1827: "There are few parts either of the *Tierra Caliente* or of the table-land in which maize is not cultivated with success. In the low hot grounds upon the coast, and on the slope of the Cordillera, its growth is more colossal than on the table-land; but even there, at seven and eight thousand feet above the level of the sea, its fecundity is such as will hardly be credited in Europe." † About twenty years later the American historian of Mexico said: "The present corn production of Mexico is not accurately determined, but it is estimated that it is the chief subsistence of at least five million persons, whilst it supplies the only fodder for all kinds of domestic animals. Its average product must, therefore, be not far from at least twenty million bushels." ‡ Since 1827 Texas declared her independence; and since the other review of Mexico was written she

---

* See his article in *New York Herald*, April 24, 1877.
† Ward's "Mexico in 1827," i. 42.
‡ Mayer's History of Mexico, ii. 55.

has made a partial development of her agricultural capacity. We will take her corn product of 1875 as perhaps a fair illustration of what the capacity of New Spain was as a whole. According to the Report of the United States Commissioner of Agriculture, Texas, in 1875, produced 31,000,000 bushels of corn, the value of which was estimated to be $25,730,000, or $8,000,000 larger than the value of the gold product of California for the same year. As corn has always been one of the staple products of New England, a comparison of the products may not be uninteresting. We take the number of bushels, and the estimated values for the same year from the same official report, viz.:

	No. of Bushels.	Value.
Maine..............	1,300,000	$1,248,000
New Hampshire...	1,650,000	1,551,000
Vermont..........	1,720,000	1,616,800
Massachusetts.....	1,620,000	1,539,000
Connecticut.......	1,775,000	1,775,000
Rhode Island.....	290,000	319,000
New York........	19,750,000	14,615,000
Total.........	28,105,000	$22,663,800

We have added the crop of New York State to the list, and find that the total value is still over three million dollars less than that of the crop of undeveloped Texas.

BARLEY.

Barley is another cereal which yields to profusion in New Spain. In proof of this assertion we will take the statistics of California for the year 1875, in comparison with the leading States of the Union in this product : *

State.	Value of Crop.
1. California	$8,235,500
2. New York	6,942,000
3. Iowa	3,339,000
4. Illinois	2,030,000
5. Wisconsin	2,024,000

Mexico, as well as the northern portion of New Spain, is peculiarly adapted to the successful growing of this commodity. As the United States imported during the year ending June 30, 1876, $7,887,886 worth of barley, and nearly as much each of the two years preceding, Mexico would do well to devote more attention to the production of this cereal.

CATTLE.

As it is impossible to find the statistics of many elements of the wealth of New Spain, as a whole, we will continue to consider Texas and California as representative States, and give such statistics as

---

* See Annual Report of Commissioner of Agriculture.

their partial development presents. If the reader thinks it is unfair to select these portions as representative of the agricultural capacity of the Southwest, as a whole, we beg leave to again call his attention to the above quoted under-estimate, twenty-seven years ago, of the capacity of California. That State, in minerals, climate, "dry regions," need of irrigation, and in other respects, bears great resemblance to Mexico; and why should not Mexico and New Spain, as a whole, bear great resemblance to California in surprising results of an agricultural development?

According to the United States census of 1870, there are three classifications of cattle, viz.: Milch cows, working oxen, and other cattle. Comparing the statistics of Texas with those of Illinois, the great State of the Mississippi Valley, we have the following:

		Numbers.
Texas:	Milch cows	428,048
	Working oxen	132,407
	Other cattle	2,933,588
Illinois:	Milch cows	640,321
	Working oxen	19,766
	Other cattle	1,055,499

Texas and Illinois are ahead of every other State in the numbers of "other cattle," and, as will be observed, Texas has three times as many as Illinois.

The total number of "other cattle" of the whole United States, in 1870, was given as 13,566,005. It will be observed that Texas possessed nearly one-fourth of this total.

California, as usual, is prepared for a comparison; and we find in the annual report for 1876 of the United States Commissioner of Agriculture, the three leading States, in "oxen and other cattle," to be as follows in numbers in January, 1877:

>   Texas...................... 3,390,500
>   Illinois...................... 1,287,000
>   California.................... 1,053,500

Perhaps no other feature of New Mexico, Northern Mexico, and, indeed, of the whole Southwest, is so well known and admitted by the outside world as its capacity for cattle-raising. It is an industry which demands, for an extensive and successful development, the same mild winters and other advantageous characteristics which the Southwest possesses.

SHEEP AND WOOL.

The Southwest has equal advantages for the raising of sheep and wool, though perhaps not as well known to the outside world. Drawing upon California once more for statistics, and for a sample of the capacity of the Southwest as a whole, we find that it was in 1870 the second State of the Union in rank in the number of sheep,

    Ohio having.............. 4,928,635, and
    California 2,768,187

These two States were also, in 1870, ahead of every other in the wool product,

    Ohio producing....... 20,539,643 lbs., and
    California............ 11,391,743 lbs.*

If we had within reach the statistics of the wool products of New Mexico for the past few years, we might give another illustration of the adaptability of the great Southwest to this important and profitable industry.

COFFEE.

Of the southern portion of New Spain, the British minister wrote, in 1827: "Coffee is another of the tropical productions for which the soil of Mexico is admirably adapted." After describing two large estates, he said they "contain about 500,000 coffee plants, 50,000 of which were in full produce when I saw them in 1826. The crop of the preceding year amounted to 5,000 arrobas, or 125,000 pounds, which gives two and a half pounds of cof-

---

* See United States Census of 1870.

fee as the average production of each plant. I am induced to believe that this will be the ordinary produce of good land throughout Mexico; it considerably exceeds that of Havana, where Humboldt gives 860 *kilogrammes* as the average of a *hectare* of land containing 3,500 plants; but it is a much lower estimate than any Mexican planter would make, as in many parts of the country from three to four pounds are said to be a fair average crop. I could not ascertain, however, that this calculation was founded upon correct data; and I do not, therefore, give it as one that may be strictly relied upon; but I know one instance of a single coffee tree having produced twenty-eight pounds of coffee in the garden of Don Pablo de la Llane, at Cordova, and it is the certainty that this fact is unquestionably true that induces me to give, as the possible average of good grounds in Mexico, a produce more than double that which in the island of Cuba is the maximum of the best year in three." *

Quite an effort has been made, in Mexico, during the past few years, to extend this profitable industry, and, judging from the reports of the United States consuls, the effort has been attended with marked success. The report of the United States Consul-General to the State Department for 1874

---

* Ward's "Mexico," i. 72 and 73.

5

contains the following: "The value of the coffee exported from Vera Cruz to the United States, during the year ending June 30, 1874, is $543,352; and it is not unreasonable to estimate, considering the home consumption, that the crop of coffee raised last year on the coffee plantations, scattered over a limited area between this city and the Gulf coast, amounts to over a million of dollars. This can be increased to a hundred millions with a comparatively small money capital and a large investment of enterprise."* The official report, from the same source, for the year 1876, shows that the export of coffee, from the single port of Vera Cruz, for the year ending June 30, 1876, was, in value, $1,146,845. As the United States imports each year, from all sources, over fifty million dollars' worth of coffee, Mexico certainly has a great inducement to develop, to their utmost capacity, her coffee plantations; and the United States would be benefited in turn by finding a good supply so near her own door.

SUGAR.

All of the standard authorities on the Mexican portion of New Spain testify to its remarkable capacity for the production of sugar. Baron Hum-

---

* See Report on Commercial Relations for 1874, p. 829.

boldt tells how, in 1553, only thirty-two years after the conquest by Cortez, the production was "so great in Mexico that it was exported from Vera Cruz and Acapulco into Spain and Peru."* In his account of that industry, at the commencement of the present century, he stated: "The cultivation of sugar-cane has made such rapid progress within these last years that the exportation of sugar at the port of Vera Cruz actually amounts to more than half a million of arrobas, or 6,250,000 kilogrammes." That reduced to pounds is 13,980,312.

Again, quoting from the report of the British minister, in 1827, we have the following testimony: "The State of Vera Cruz alone is capable of supplying all Europe with sugar. Humboldt estimates the produce of its richest mould at 2,800 *kilogrammes* per *hectare*, while that of Cuba does not exceed 1,400 kilogrammes, so that the balance is as two to one in favor of Vera Cruz."† About twenty years later, Mayer, the historian of Mexico, wrote: "The sugar-cane is one of the most valuable agricultural products of Mexico, and we are convinced, from personal observation, that the estates in the *Tierra Caliente*, where it is chiefly raised, are the richest as well as the most beautiful in the

---

* See Humboldt's "New Spain," iii. 4.
† Ward's "Mexico," i. 21.

republic."* Still later authority is the report of the United States Consul from the State of Vera Cruz in 1874. He says: "The sugar-cane once planted lasts from fifteen to twenty years, and this with the very little care that is given it by the Mexicans generally. It is supposed that the same planting will last even for a longer time when cultivated with the intelligence and experience of the foreign planter." †

Again, in 1875, a consul of the United States reported: "The plantations in the State of Morelos (adjoining the States of Mexico and Puebla), and which are over some forty in number, now produce far more than is required for home consumption, and are capable of increasing their products three or four-fold." ‡

The exports of sugar from Mexico are evidently but a small portion of the product, and the exports from the single port of Vera Cruz are not all of the exports. But as we are unable to find satisfactory information in regard to the amount raised, we give the following table of exports of sugar from Vera Cruz, for the past few years, as some indication of an increased development of that industry in Mexico.§

---

* Mayer's History of Mexico, ii. 62.
† See Report on Commercial Relations for 1874, p. 876.
‡ Idem, for 1875, p. 1118.
§ Idem, for 1876, p. 746.

Years ending June 30.	Value in Dollars.
1872–1873	40
1873–1874	1,884
1874–1875	25,161
1875–1876	228,832

COCHINEAL.

Another striking illustration of the assertion that silver and gold do not comprise all the wealth of New Spain are the statistics in regard to the product of cochineal. Ward speaks of it as a product "which nature seems to have bestowed almost exclusively upon Mexico; for the insect which bears the same name in the Brazils is a very inferior kind." He states that "the plantations of the cochineal cactus are confined to the district of La Misteca, in the State of Oaxaca." After telling how, in 1758, a government registry of this important industry was established in the above-mentioned State, he says: "By the official returns, which I possess, it appears that the value of cochineal entered upon the books of this office, up to 1815, was $91,308,907, which, upon fifty-seven years, gives an average of $1,601,910 per annum, without making any allowance for contraband."* He estimated the contraband as one-fourth more, and consequently the average annual value to be $2,002,387. Mayer

---

* Ward's "Mexico," i. 84, 85.

gives the statistics of the product down to 1832 as follows: "It appears that from 1758 to 1832, inclusive, or in seventy-five years, 44,195,750 pounds of cochineal were produced in the State of Oajaca alone, which were worth $106,170,671 at the market price." *

SILK.

The raising of silk cocoons was, many years ago, quite an industry in parts of New England, and many a fine field was covered with mulberry-trees, the leaves of which furnished food for the worms. But little remains of that industry there except the stumps of the trees. It has reappeared in New Spain, and has been accompanied there with marked success. Of the 3,937 pounds of silk cocoons raised in the United States, in 1870, 3,587 pounds were raised in California.† Brace, who wrote about 1868, says of the mulberry-trees: "Some 4,000,000 trees are said already to have been planted in the State." ‡

QUICKSILVER.

In a careful review of the mineral products of the United States during its first century, Prof. Hunt says of California, one of the States of for-

---

* See his History of Mexico.
† See United States Census of 1870.
‡ "The New West," by C. L. Brace, p. 323.

mer New Spain: "In no other region of the globe, however, is the ore of quicksilver so widely distributed as in California, and there is reason to believe that from the opening and working of new deposits the production will soon be much increased, a result which will be stimulated by the present high price of quicksilver, and its scarcity in foreign markets."* Another authority states that it "is found at many localities in Mexico, but is not extracted at present on a large scale."† The value of the exports of quicksilver in California from 1852 (about the beginning of the working of the mines) to 1867, has been estimated to be $16,000,000.‡ The United States Commissioner of Mining Statistics, in his annual report for 1874, estimates California's exports of quicksilver, for the period 1859 to 1874, both inclusive, to be $14,226,441.

FRUITS AND WINES.

Many portions of the Southwest produce delicate and semi-tropical fruits, and the finest quality of wine. Many other portions are well adapted in climate and soil to the successful prosecution of that industry. In the hot, or low lands of Mexico, the banana, orange, pine-apple, and lemon, of excellent

---

* "First Century of the Republic," p. 199.
† See paper on Mercury, in American Cyclopædia.
‡ See Blake on "Production of Precious Metals," p. 196.

quality, are produced in abundance. Ward says: "The banana is to the inhabitants of the *Tierra Caliente* what maize is to those of the table land; it furnishes them with the principal article of their daily food." * In Central New Spain, near the boundary between the two republics, fruits and wines of remarkable richness grow in great profusion. The grape of the Messila valley, in Southern New Mexico, is noted for its fine qualities. In Southern California the new civilization, which has been developing that State since the discovery of gold, is showing to the outside world some significant facts and figures in regard to the capabilities of New Spain in the growing of fruits and wines. A recent writer, in a description of one of the estates in Southern California, says: "Standing on the front veranda one looks down a broad avenue overshadowed on each side by magnificent orange-trees. This is *par excellence* the orange avenue. It extends a mile with double rows of trees on each side. Mr. Rose has, in all, between six and seven thousand orange-trees, but only a comparatively small part of them have come into bearing. He has one hundred and fifty acres in vineyards, wherein grow one hundred and thirty-five thousand vines, from which he made last year one hundred thou-

---

* Ward's "Mexico," i. 51.

sand gallons of white wine and three thousand gallons of brandy. A part of the crop that he sent to the market last year consisted of two hundred and fifty thousand oranges, fifty thousand lemons, and twenty-five thousand pounds of English walnuts. Besides these tropical fruits, he raises apples, pears, and peaches in considerable quantities, and in addition to all these, pomegranates, figs, nectarines, apricots, and olives." * The same author speaks of another orange grove in Southern California " containing two thousand trees, which, when sixteen years old, averaged one thousand five hundred oranges per tree, and has continued to yield about the same each year;" of still another orange grove of sixteen hundred and fifty trees, some of which have borne as many as four thousand oranges; of a gentleman in Los Angeles who "in 1873 sold twelve hundred dollars' worth of oranges from the trees on half an acre;" of "an olive-tree in Santa Barbara, that is thirty years old, from which has been made forty-eight dollars' worth of oil each year, for three successive years." The author also states that there are "twenty thousand olive-trees already set out in Southern California." † Another writer on California says : "There are pear-trees at San José which produce twenty-five hundred pounds, or forty

---

* " Two Years in California," by Mary Cone, p. 65.
† Idem, pp. 65, 85, and 86.

bushels each of fruit annually." * Still another authority on California, in describing the great vineyards of that State as he saw them about 1868, estimated the number of grape-vines in Sonoma valley to be 2,438,000.† In the United States census of 1870 the wine production is given both in the statistics of agriculture and manufactures, " according as the wine is made upon the farm or vineyard, and consequently by agricultural labor or in large establishments." On the farms California produced 1,814,656 gallons of the total 3,092,330 gallons produced in the whole United States, and was the first State of the Union in that product, the second State, which was Missouri, producing only 326,173 gallons. Of the amount *manufactured* California furnished a product worth $602,553. Only one State manufactured more, and that was Missouri, whose product was worth $934,442.

The total wine product of California, for the year 1876, is estimated to be $3,000,000, and the value of the fruit product $2,500,000.‡

RÉSUMÉ.

The above elements of wealth, other than silver and gold, are not all of the varied resources of New

---

* Hittel's "California," p. 191.
† "The New West," by C. L. Brace, p. 261.
‡ San Francisco *Journal of Commerce*, January 10, 1877.

Spain. But the few facts and figures given are sufficient to prove that the Southwest is as rich in agriculture as in precious metals. Of the States of the Union the first in silver, gold, wheat, barley, silk, cattle, are States acquired from Mexico, and within the limits of New Spain. Furthermore, one of the States in the same remarkable area will very soon be first in the value of its cotton product, for Texas, *on less than one per cent. of its area*, produced, in 1876, more than any other State, except Mississippi.

Remarkable as are these statistics, they are still more so when we consider that the Southwest is comparatively new to American civilization, is sparsely settled, is almost unknown to railways, and comparatively undeveloped.

Probably no other portion of the earth's surface is naturally so self-supporting, for the long list of its products not only embraces the staple articles of commerce and the necessities of life, but also very many of the luxuries; and all grow in great profusion.

CHAPTER IV.

LUXURIES AND ATTRACTIONS.

FACILITIES FOR THE ACQUIREMENT OF WEALTH.

THE country which abounds in facilities for the acquisition of wealth, as well as its enjoyment, is pre-eminently the place for luxuries. Such a land is New Spain. Without riches in silver and gold and agriculture, it would be an attractive resort for tourists and pleasure-seekers from abroad, because of its delightful climate, high table-lands, and magnificent scenery. But climate and scenery are not sufficient for the wants of permanent inhabitants. The world is full of illustrations of the tendency, on the part of the rich, to leave the unattractive places where they were enabled to acquire fortunes, and go elsewhere with their riches, seeking pleasures and luxuries. Fortunate is the country which furnishes both riches and pleasures. The immense treasures in silver and gold of the Montezumas, the great wealth acquired by many of the Spanish proprietors of the mines in Old Mexico, the princely fortunes unlocked from the mines of California and Nevada, in the northern portion of New Spain, are striking instances of the capacity of the Southwest, as a whole, when, as a whole, it receives an adequate development. Cortez undertook the conquest of Mexico because he believed it to be a promising field for the acquirement of riches. That he did not overestimate the wealth of that portion of New Spain appears from the amount of spoils secured by his soldiers, the known value of which was over six million dollars, and the value of that not estimated by the historians was perhaps as much more. We have already seen how one of the Spanish miners of Durango extracted thirty million dollars in precious metals in the space of twenty-four years; how in the north of New Spain over a thousand millions of gold have been taken from the mines of California since 1848, and nearly three hundred millions of gold and silver taken from the mines of Nevada since 1859. According to the United States census the value of real and personal property of California, at different dates, is estimated as follows:

  1850..................... $22,161,872
  1860..................... 207,874,613
  1870..................... 638,767,017

Of the history of material development, the world has never furnished so brilliant a page as

California during the last twenty-nine years. It is unnecessary to mention individual instances of the fortunes acquired in California and Nevada, for the story has many times been told, and is well known. Suffice it to say that San Francisco in a very few years has grown to be an important money center, and the great fortunes of the future in this country are likely to be most numerous on the Pacific coast.

TOPOGRAPHY AND CLIMATE.

Good climate is not only one of the greatest of luxuries, but is an absolute necessity for thousands of suffering humanity. It is a luxury which, in itself, costs no money, but immense sums are spent every year in the pilgrimage to find it. Business is neglected, and expense disregarded by those whose lives depend upon the pure, dry, and exhilarating air of high elevations, and an escape from the severity of northern winters. All of these good qualities may be found in the climate of New Spain to a degree unsurpassed by any other part of the world. Florida possesses some of these qualities, but not the elevations or dryness. Other resorts are elevated and dry, but without mild winters. In the Southwest all of these features are combined. Large numbers of health-seekers have already been attracted to Southern Colorado, New Mexico, Arizona, and Southern California, and when that region is more generally known to the outside world, and the advance of railways renders it more accessible, thousands more will seek its health-giving climate.

As we have previously seen, the great interior of Old Mexico is a highly elevated table-land, and New Mexico averages 5,660 feet above the sea. A good authority states that "the Mexicans divide their country, with respect to climate, into Tierras Calientes (hot lands), which rarely exceed 900 feet in elevation; Tierras Templadas (temperate), ranging between 4,000 and 5,000 feet; and Tierras Frias (cold), above 7,000 feet." * Of these classifications the hot lands constitute a very small portion of the area, and are the narrow strip of low elevations near the oceans. A writer on New Mexico makes the following comment on its climate, which could with equal justice be applied to Old Mexico, viz.: "The sanitoria of the Union is located in Southern New Mexico, where the atmosphere is more dry than in Colorado, the sky brighter, the nights sufficiently cool for refreshing sleep, and free from 'damp night air,' and the elevations are such as to suit each case, varying from the elevation of the Rio Grande at 4,000 feet, to the mines in Grant County, and the high cattle

---

* Paper on Mexico in Lippincott's Gazetteer.

ranches in the Guadaloupe ranges in Lincoln County, where 7,000 feet may be selected on the clear trout streams and cool springs of water." *

An authority on "Semi-tropical California" says of Los Angeles: "During what may be termed the winter months 50° will mark on an average the mean temperature, and water is never congealed."† It gives for the year 1871, the temperature of a place in Los Angeles as follows: ‡

Month.	Sunrise.	9 A.M.	3 P.M.	9 P.M.
January	40	55	64	50
February	41	56	64	48
March	40	60	69	54
April	53	66	73	57
May	56	65	71	60
June	61	70	77	64
July	66	74	80	67
August	65	75	81	69
September	61	75	85	67
October	59	74	79	62
November	49	67	69	57
December	47	57	62	51

Prof. Raymond, in his annual report for 1870, says: "The climate of New Mexico is mild and

---

* "New Mexico," by Brevoort, p. 149.
† Truman's "Semi-tropical California," p. 31.
‡ Idem, p. 78.

healthy, the sky as clear as that of Italy, and the air transparent and pure. In fact the very act of breathing in this country makes existence in it a pleasure." *

But the pure mountain air of the Southwest is not confined to the uninhabited regions. Many of the business centers and great cities are mountain cities, Santa Fé, in New Mexico, being 7,047 feet above the sea, and the capital of Old Mexico 7,469 feet above the sea. Those who dread the fogs and miasmas of river valleys, the severe winters of New England and other Northern States, who seek a mild, agreeable, and invigorating climate, either as a necessity or luxury, can find it in the land selected by the civilized native races as their mountain home, coveted and conquered by the Spanish, and now being approached by the Anglo-American civilization.

SCENERY AND WONDERS.

Perhaps not in the whole world can the pleasure-seekers find a greater variety of wonders and magnificent scenery than in different portions of New Spain. An elevated mountain city possesses the luxury of grand scenery as well as delightful climate. Mexico is in the mountains, over seven

---

* Annual Report on Mining Statistics, p. 383.

thousand feet above the sea, and also in a valley surrounded by mountains. In other words, it is situated in a mountain valley which is surrounded by mountain ranges and peaks, making a rare combination of remarkable scenery. The valley of Mexico, as first seen by the Spanish conquerors, when on their march they reached the summit of the surrounding mountains, is beautifully illustrated by the word-painting of Prescott as follows: " Its picturesque assemblage of water, woodland, and cultivated plains, its shining cities and shadowy hills, was spread out like some gay and gorgeous panorama before them. In the highly rarefied atmosphere of these upper regions even remote objects have a brilliancy of coloring and a distinctness of outline which seem to annihilate distance. Stretching far away at their feet were seen noble forests of oak, sycamore, and cedar ; and beyond, yellow fields of maize, and the towering maguey intermingled with orchards and blooming gardens ; for flowers, in such demand for their religious festivals, were even more abundant in this populous valley than in other parts of Anahuac. In the center of the great basin were beheld the lakes, occupying then a much larger portion of its surface than at present ; their borders thickly studded with towns and hamlets in the midst—like some Indian empress with her coronal of pearls,—the fair city of

Mexico, with her white towers and pyramidal temples reposing as it were on the bosom of the waters, the far-famed 'Venice of the Aztecs.'"* The city and lakes have changed since the days of the conquest, but in other respects the magnificence of the combination of mountain and valley remains the same.

As we have previously stated, this is not a detailed review of the Southwest. It is a brief statistical summary, and space does not permit more than a few notes on the subject of scenery. The Yosemite Valley, in northern New Spain, would alone require a whole volume, with costly illustrations. Such works are already in existence, and are mentioned in the list of "Authorities." There are, however, a few wonders which can appropriately be noticed here, and one is the "big trees." Bancroft speaks of nine groves having been discovered in California, of which the most remarkable are those known as Calaveras and Mariposa groves. He says, of Calaveras grove, that it "contains about ninety trees, which can be called really big;" and then proceeds to give the measurement of all of the thirty-one which had been measured by the State survey.† This list contains—

---

* Prescott's "Conquest of Mexico," ii. 51, 52.
† Bancroft's "Tourist's Guide," pp. 52–54.

Five between 231 and 250 feet high.
Seventeen between 250 and 275 feet high.
Five   "   275 " 300   "
Three   "   300 " 325   "

and one 325 feet high, with a girth of 45 feet six feet from the ground. Of another one of this list, he states it had a girth of 61 feet, without the bark.

Of Mariposa grove he says that there were, at the time of the last official count, 606 trees. Of the two groves he says: "Both the Calaveras and Mariposa groves contain hollow trunks of fallen trees through which two, and even three horsemen can ride abreast for 60 or 70 feet."*

Of the age of the trees, Whitney, in his "Geological Survey of California," states that one of the trees in the Calaveras grove, "six feet above the ground, has a diameter of 23 feet inside the bark, and was found to be about 1,300 years old. It was easy to count the annual rings, and they amounted to 1,255 in number; but there being a small space, about a foot in diameter, at the center of the tree, from which the wood was decayed away, it would be a reasonable estimate to call the age of this particular tree about 1,300 years." †

But mountain cities, "big trees," and the won-

---

* Idem, p. 62.
† Whitney's "Geological Survey of California," i. 444.

derful Yosemite Valley are not all. Brace describes a grape-vine near Santa Barbara, in California, which "was planted by a lady, Donna de Dominguez, over sixty-five years ago, from a slip which she had cut in Monterey County for a horsewhip. It is trained on a trellis, about ten feet from the ground, and now covers a space, as I measured it, of ninety-three feet by about fifty. The circumference of the trunk five inches from the ground was three feet and a half inch ; and eight feet high, just below the branches, it measured four feet and three inches. It bears about eight thousand pounds of grapes per annum, and is said to almost support the family which own it."* Another wonder, according to Baron Humboldt, and which we have already described, is the highly elevated plateau or flattened crest of the mountains extending through the center of New Spain, and which he considered one of the most remarkable formations of the kind in the whole world.

Still another remarkable formation is the cañon of the Colorado River of the West, and one which has not a parallel in the whole world. The rocky walls, between which this river flows, are, at one place, 6,200 feet high, rising almost perpendicularly. In other words, the walls which stand facing each

---

* " The New West," by C. L. Brace, pp. 302, 303.

other on opposite sides of the narrow stream are over a mile high." *

ANTIQUITIES.

To the student there is no greater pleasure than a visit to the ancient ruins of the classic nations. In his college course the study of Ancient America has been sacrificed for the study of Ancient Greece and Rome. It is not unreasonable that the study of the antiquities of foreign civilized nations should be more attractive and instructive than the antiquities of wild Indian tribes at home. But there is one portion of North America which abounds in antiquities of a very brilliant civilization, and another portion which abounds in the ruins of semi-civilized native races. Both of these classes of antiquities are confined to New Spain, the ruins of the Aztecs, Toltecs, and perhaps still earlier nations being in Old Mexico, and the ruins of the Pueblos in New Mexico and Arizona and other portions of the territory acquired from Mexico. To describe these ruins would require, at least, a dozen volumes larger than this, and to illustrate them would require a fortune of large dimensions. Lord Kingsborough's illustrated work on Mexican antiquities, as we have already mentioned, cost over one hundred and sixty thousand dollars. We can only

---

* See Powell on the Colorado River of the West.

mention a few significant facts and figures, and call the attention of the reader to the authorities on this subject, to show that it is one of the great attractions of New Spain. And it is an attraction which will be appreciated when there are such railway facilities as will enable the student and tourist to conveniently visit that part of classic America.

Of Yucatan, the southern State of New Spain, Bancroft states it "presents a rich field for antiquarian exploration, furnishing, perhaps, finer and certainly more numerous specimens of ancient aboriginal architecture, sculpture, and painting than have been discovered in any other section of America. The State is literally dotted, at least in the northern, central, or best known portions, with ruined edifices and cities." * Stephens, who was the first one to make an extensive exploration of Yucatan, and whose two interesting volumes that record his discoveries contain one hundred and twenty engravings illustrating the ruins, says: "In our long, irregular, and devious route, we have discovered the crumbling remains of forty-four ancient cities, most of them but a short distance apart." † Many of these ruins will compare favorably with the ruins of the European classic nations, as a reference to illustrations contained in Ste-

---

* Bancroft's "Native Races," iv. 143.
† Stephens on Yucatan, ii. 444.

phens's, Lord Kingsborough's, Catherwood's, and other works will prove.

The *Casa del Gobernador*, one of the buildings described and illustrated in these works, was "a building three hundred and twenty-two feet long, thirty-nine feet wide, and twenty-six feet high, built of stone and mortar." * Coming northwardly through New Spain, one can find, between Vera Cruz and the city of Mexico, the ruins of a pyramid of "sandstone in regularly cut blocks laid in mortar," seven stories high, and over ninety feet square at the base.† In about the same latitude, and not far from the present city of Puebla, are the ruins of the pyramid of Cholula. It is thus described by Bancroft: "From a base about fourteen hundred and forty feet square, whose sides face the cardinal points, it rose in four equal stories to a height of nearly two hundred feet, having a summit platform of about two hundred feet square." * * * "It is very evident that the pyramid of Cholula contains nothing in itself to indicate its age, but from well-defined and doubtless reliable traditions, we may feel very sure that its erection dates back to the tenth century, and probably preceding the seventh. Humboldt shows that it is larger at the base than any of the old-

---

* Bancroft's "Native Races," iv. 156.
† Idem, pp. 452-454.

world pyramids—over twice as large as that of Cheops." *

The broad platform at the summit of this pyramid was, says the historian, arranged for a temple, which was several times built and rebuilt, its last destruction being at the hands of the soldiers of Cortez in a fierce battle with the Aztecs.

Still farther north, near the boundary between the United States and Mexico, are ruins of the semi-civilization. They are described in detail and finely illustrated by the engravings of Bartlett's elaborate work on the border States.

As we have already mentioned, Coronado, who explored the northern portion of New Spain soon after Cortez conquered Mexico, found in New Mexico, Arizona, and Southern Colorado, seventy ancient cities or villages, and ruins of many more.† According to Davis, some of the buildings among those ruins contained six and seven stories.‡

In the extreme northern portion of New Spain, as well as the southern and central portions, the ancient ruins are very abundant, so much so, that Holmes, of Prof. Hayden's survey, in his recent report on the ruins of the San Juan region, chiefly in Southwestern Colorado, states: "There is boun-

---

* Idem, pp. 469–475.
† Ante, p. 13.
‡ Ante, p. 12.

tiful evidence that at one time it supported a numerous population; there is scarcely a square mile in the six thousand examined that would not furnish evidence of occupation by a race totally distinct from the nomadic savages who hold it now, and in every way superior to them." *

In support of the assertion that New Spain is exceedingly attractive in its antiquities, and that the ancient ruins and architecture will compare very favorably with those of foreign classic nations, we invite the attention of the reader to the magnificent illustrations of Mexican monuments in Lord Kingsborough's costly work, to the equally magnificent but less costly illustrations by Catherwood, to the many views of the massive ruins of Yucatan contained in Stephens's profusely illustrated work, and to the thorough and comprehensive reviews of the antiquities of New Spain contained in Baldwin's "Ancient America," and the fourth volume of Bancroft's "Native Races."

In view of the fact that the ancient history of the Southwest is a history of civilization, that the only ancient civilization of North America was confined to that particular section, the study of its antiquities is very important as well as attractive.

The new interest in the ancient history of Amer-

---

* See paper on ancient ruins of Southwestern Colorado, by W. H. Holmes, in tenth annual report of Hayden's Survey.

ica, stimulated by Bancroft's recent and complete review of the native races of New Spain, by the recent explorations of, and reports on, the antiquities by Prof. Hayden's and Lieutenant Wheeler's Surveys, and by the recent Centennial of American Independence, makes the Southwest, which is the richest field for such researches, unusually conspicuous. And when New Spain is intersected by railways, we may expect to see frequent pilgrimages of patriotic Americans to that shrine of ancient American history.

FLOWERS.

New Spain might with propriety have been called the Flowery Kingdom, for the march of the Spanish soldiers under Cortez, from the coast to the interior, was along a pathway of flowers, a luxury comparatively unknown to the other pioneers from Europe who entered America on the shores of New England. The historian, in describing the march from Vera Cruz toward the capital, tells how, when they arrived at Cempoalla, " the women, as well as the men, mingled fearlessly among the soldiers, bearing bunches and wreaths of flowers, with which they decorated the neck of the general's charger, and hung a chaplet of roses about his helmet. Flowers were the delight of this people. They bestowed much care in their cultivation."* Again, in describing the entrance to Cholula, in the interior, the historian says the native people "showed the same delicate taste for flowers as the other tribes of the plateau, decorating their persons with them, and tossing garlands and bunches among the soldiers."† Still more interesting is the description of the great market at the Aztec capital. Prescott, after speaking of the various products and wares exhibited there for sale, says: "All these commodities, and every stall and portico were set out, or rather smothered with flowers, showing, on a much larger scale indeed, a taste similar to that displayed in the markets of modern Mexico. Flowers seem to be the spontaneous growth of this luxuriant soil, which, instead of noxious weeds, as in other regions, is ever ready, without the aid of man, to cover up its nakedness with this rich and variegated livery of nature."‡ Mexico of the present day abounds in this pleasing luxury. A recent authority states that "the flowers of Mexico are among the richest and most varied in the world, and several of the streets of the capital on Sunday mornings are literally enameled with flowers of brilliant hue and fragrant odor."§ Northern New

---

* Prescott's "Conquest of Mexico," i. 342.
† Idem, ii. 13.   ‡ Idem, p. 138.
§ Paper on Mexico in American Cyclopædia.

Spain, as well as the Mexican portion, possesses the same attractive features in the profusion of flowers. In his review of California, Brace says: "San Francisco should be called the 'City of Flowers.' Such is the power of this divine climate, that it only needs a little patch of sand and mould, with plenty of water, to produce the most magnificent vegetation. Every house with bits of yard like ours in New York makes the most splendid show of flowers; scarlet geraniums ten feet high, lemon verbenas which are small trees, fuchsias of immense size, callas in great bunches, splendid roses of many varieties, clambering vines, large cacti, gum-trees (*Eucalypti*) of Australia, and beautiful evergreens from Japan, Australia, and this coast—all left out through the year, and only needing plenty of water from the garden hose." *

With such an array of testimony, and much more which might be cited to the same effect, the term "Flowery Kingdom" seems particularly appropriate.

FRUITS AND WINES.

Perhaps the tropical fruits and delicate wines of New Spain are quite as important as luxuries as an element of wealth; and what there is on this

---

* The "New West," by C. L. Brace, p. 37.

subject in the preceding chapter could with propriety be reproduced here. Most all of the leading markets in the United States which deal in imported luxuries are supplied with the pears and grapes and wines of California. Oranges, olives, pineapples, bananas, and figs are other luxuries which grow in profusion in New Spain, but thus far have been enjoyed chiefly by her own inhabitants. The tropical and semi-tropical regions of the Southwest can, with suitable development, supply the whole of North America with these luxuries, so extensively imported and used.

LUXURIOUS LIVING.

Other lands are attractive because of the grandeur of scenery, the wonders of nature, and the antiquities; but, as a rule, they are not wealth-producing, and the attractions are consequently mainly enjoyed by the tourists from abroad. New Spain possesses a great advantage in the combination of natural wealth and luxuries. It is a place for luxurious living at home. It was so in the days of the Montezumas, and is so to a remarkable degree under the civilization which has started its modern development in California. "Solomon in all his glory was not arrayed" more gorgeously than the king of the Aztecs; nor were the presents from the

Queen of Sheba to King Solomon as great in value as those from Montezuma to Cortez.

Bancroft states that Montezuma changed his dress four times each day, and a dress worn once could never be used again.*

The same historian says, in his description of Montezuma's palace: "The dinner-service was of the finest ware of Cholula, and many of the goblets were of gold and silver, or fashioned of beautiful shells. He is said to have possessed a complete set of solid gold; but as it was considered below a king's dignity to use anything at table twice, Montezuma, with all his extravagance, was obliged to keep this costly dinner-set in the temple. The bill of fare comprised everything edible of fish, flesh, and fowl that could be procured in the empire or imported from beyond it." † No country but one rich in resources would beget the luxurious customs so prevalent in the Aztec civilization. Bancroft says: "The excessive fondness of the Aztecs for feasts and amusements of every kind, seems to have extended through all ranks of society. Every man feasted his neighbor, and was himself in turn feasted. Birthdays, victories, house-warmings, successful voyages or speculations, and other events too numerous to enumerate were celebrated with

---

* " Native Races," ii. 179.
† Bancroft's " Native Races," ii. 174, 175.

feasts. Every man, from king to peasant, considered it incumbent upon him to be second to none among his equals in the giving of banquets and entertainments."* Young nations seldom enjoy the same degree of luxury that has been attained by older ones, where wealth has accumulated. A large portion of the first century of the United States, as well as many previous years of colonial experience, was unaccompanied by luxurious living. The New England settlers had to do chiefly with the trials, privations, the stern realities and prose of life; and what luxuries are now enjoyed by their descendants were of exceedingly slow growth. But the character of the soil and climate of New England, more than its youth, was the barrier to luxurious living, as the short experience and rapid attainment of wealth and luxury of California most conclusively proves. Had the energetic and thrifty Pilgrims entered America in the Southwest instead of the Northeast, the early history of this country would have been far more brilliant. Now the Anglo-American civilization has extended across the continent, with its accumulation of experience and skill, and has commenced operations on the borders of New Spain, it will be an interesting spectacle to watch the results. It is

---

* Bancroft's "Native Races," ii. 283.

reasonable to presume the development will be more prolific in luxuries than any portion of North America, outside of New Spain, has ever known.

During the past few years much has been said by the press of this country about the annual exodus to Europe of the rich, the tourists, and pleasure-seekers, and the amount of money spent there each year by Americans has been estimated to be very many millions of dollars. The remedy proposed is to make home more attractive. But money spent on improvements will not change the New England climate or that of river valleys; nor will it create mountain scenery where it does not already exist. The true way to prevent the continual outflow of capital is to develop that portion of America where nature has provided luxuries in great abundance; and New Spain is endowed to profusion with the many qualities which add luxury to life.

6*

CHAPTER V.

THE AUTHORITIES.

The Southwest, or New Spain, is as rich in written history as in silver and gold. It has furnished the world with as many volumes as the Northeast, or New England. But a glance at the book-shelves of libraries in the United States does not confirm this assertion, for the reason that the larger portion were published in Spanish and are not generally translated or known in this country. Again, of the many books in English on Mexico, a large portion were published in England, and many of them are little known in America. The Library of Congress, however, is an exception, for it contains nearly every work in English which has ever been published on Mexico, or the States and Territories of the cessions to the United States. There may be a few other libraries which contain nearly complete sets of English authorities on New Spain, but these collections are not sufficiently numerous or accessible to answer the wants of the business community, which is being attracted more than ever before toward the great Southwest and its material development. Authorities are coming into demand, but are difficult to find. Books on some distant foreign lands are probably more generally known in this country than those on Mexico, and for the reason that the business intercourse between the two republics has been very limited. Mexico's chief want is to be known, and when it is thoroughly known to the Anglo-Americans, her wonderful riches and attractions will attract the much-needed thrifty civilization.

The books written in, or translated into, English are the only ones of much practical value to the business community; but a brief description of the books of the native races and their conquerors, the Spanish, may not be uninteresting.

Bancroft, in describing the Aztec system of writing, says that they "derived their system traditionally from the Toltecs, whose written annals they also inherited." * Humboldt says: "The Mexicans were in possession of annals that went back to eight centuries and a half beyond the epocha of the arrival of Cortez in the country of Anahuac." † We have seen, in the chapter on silver and gold, how proficient the Toltecs were in the arts, and it is to be presumed that their advanced civilization reached as far as their records and histories. For-

---

* "Natives Races of Pacific States," ii. 528.
† See Baron Humboldt's "Researches in America," p. 297.

tunately we find more information about the records of the Aztecs. Prescott says: "At the time of the arrival of the Spaniards great quantities of these manuscripts were treasured up in the country; numerous persons were employed in painting, and the dexterity of their operations excited the astonishment of the conquerors. Unfortunately this was mingled with other and unworthy feelings. The strange, unknown characters inscribed on them excited suspicion." * * * "The first archbishop of Mexico collected these paintings from every quarter, especially from Tezcuco, the most cultivated capital in Anahuac, and the great depository of the national archives. He then caused them to be piled up in a 'mountain heap,' as it is called by the Spanish writers themselves, in the market-place of Tlateloco, and reduced them all to ashes." * He further says of the Aztec manuscripts: "They were sometimes done up into rolls, but more frequently into volumes of moderate size, in which the paper was shut up like a folding screen, with a leaf or tablet of wood at each extremity that gave the whole, when closed, the appearance of a book." † Bancroft says of the Aztec books: "Respecting the historical value of the destroyed documents, it is safe to believe that they contained all that the

---

* "Conquest of Mexico," by Prescott, i. 101.
† Idem, i. 100.

Aztecs knew of their past. Having once conceived the idea of recording their annals, and having a system of writing adequate to the purpose, it is inconceivable that they failed to record all they knew." *

Lord Kingsborough's remarkable illustrated work on the antiquities of Mexico contains fac-similes of about a dozen of these Aztec books, or original hieroglyphic paintings. They contain about seventy-five pages each. A glance at them is sufficient to satisfy one that the native races were quite proficient in the making of records and histories, and that if we had access to all the books they wrote a flood of light would be let in upon the ancient history of the Southwest. The destruction of this classic history of North America is a loss which is more keenly felt now that the historians are striving to trace back, as far as possible, the history of the early civilization of a nation which is to-day one of the leading ones of the earth.

The Spanish were very prolific writers, and during their supremacy in New Spain, from the Conquest in 1521 to their downfall in 1821, furnished the world with a vast number of volumes on that attractive country. Some few have been translated, but the most are still in Spanish, and inaccessible

---

* " Native Races of Pacific States," ii. 528.

to the general reader. Bancroft's account of his own collection, made while preparing his most valuable work on the "Native Races of the Pacific States," shows how numerous are the works in Spanish. He says, in the introduction to his history: "To some it may be of interest to know the nature and extent of the author's resources for writing so important a series of works. The books and manuscripts necessary for the task existed in no library in the world; hence, in 1859, he commenced collecting material relative to the Pacific States. After securing everything in his reach in America, he twice visited Europe, spending about two years in thorough researches in England and the chief cities of the continent. Having exhausted every available source, he was obliged to content himself with lying in wait for opportunities. Not long afterward, and at a time when the prospect of materially adding to his collection seemed anything but hopeful, the *Biblioteca Imperial de Mejico* of the unfortunate Maximilian, collected during a period of forty years, by Don José Maria Andrade, *litterateur* and publisher, of the city of Mexico, was thrown on the European market, and furnished him about three thousand additional volumes. In 1869, having accumulated some sixteen thousand books, manuscripts, and pamphlets, besides maps and cumbersome files of Pacific coast journals, he determined to go to work."*

Of this collection a large number are in Spanish; and as the work is mainly on the native races who inhabited the same country which afterward constituted New Spain, a large portion of the collection must necessarily relate to the Southwest. Large as is this library, it would be much more extensive if it contained all the Spanish books and manuscripts on the various portions of New Spain. The historian of Texas expresses the opinion that there are in existence many authorities in Spanish on that State which he was unable to obtain, viz.: " The correspondence of the Franciscan Friars from 1716 to 1794 is believed to be in the parent convents of Queretaro and Zacatecas. This would throw a flood of light upon that subject." Second, " The thirty folio volumes covering the transactions in Texas, for the first half century of its history, were forwarded to the king of Spain in 1744, and are probably in the archives of Salamanca, in Spain." † As the Southwest increases in civilization and wealth, these old Spanish records and manuscripts will be more and more sought for, and it is to be hoped some American institution will yet possess a full set of Spanish authorities.

---

* From Preface of " Native Races," i.
† See introduction to Yoakum's " History of Texas."

But the works in English are the ones of greatest practical value. The following list of authorities is probably nearly all the works yet published in the English language on the history, resources, voyages, expeditions, and surveys and antiquities of New Spain. But it does not embrace all the books on the Indian tribes, town and city history, works on the war between the United States and Mexico, legislative documents, pamphlets, Mormon history of Utah—the northern state of New Spain—nor the various reports on the proposed Tehuantepec interoceanic canal across the southern State of New Spain. With a very few exceptions, all of the books in the list are to be found in the Library of Congress. As but few of the other public libraries of the United States contain complete, or even nearly complete sets of authorities on the Southwest, the names of the publishers of the respective publications are given in the list.

All of the books mentioned in the list, except the few designated by a star following the name of the author, have been examined, and the titles taken from the title-pages. The few thus designated, and which we have been unable to find, are nearly all English publications, and the names and titles are taken from the English and British catalogues of publications:

THE AUTHORITIES ON MEXICO.

Abbott, Gorham D.—Mexico and the United States. New York, 1869. G. P. Putnam & Son. It treats of the Catholic church; the government; Juarez and his cabinet; interoceanic canals; the Monroe doctrine; and gives a copy of the Constitution of Mexico.

Alarchon, Fernando.—Voyage along the Gulf of California in 1540. In Hakluyt's Voyages, iii. 505.

Alvensleben, Max, Baron Von.—With Maximilian in Mexico. London, 1867. Longmans, Green & Co.

Barinetti, C.—A Voyage to Mexico and Havana. New York, 1841. Printed for author.

Baz, Gustavo, and E. L. Gallo.—History of the Mexican Railway. Mexico, 1876. Gallo & Co.

Beaufoy, Mark.—Mexican Illustrations. London, 1828. Carpenter & Son.

Bishop, Anna.—Travels in Mexico, 1849. Philadelphia, Charles Deall. This chiefly on society of Mexico.

Browne, J. Ross.—A sketch of the settlement and exploration of Lower California. In his book on " The Resources of the Pacific States."

Bullock, W. H.—Across Mexico, in 1864-1865. London, 1866. McMillan & Co.

Bullock, W.—Six Months' Residence and Travels in Mexico. 2 vols. London, 1825. John Murray.

It contains a fine illustration of the valley and city of Mexico.

Calderon de la Barca, Madame.—Life in Mexico. London, 1843. Chapman & Hall. 2 vols. Is descriptive of Mexican society, and a leading work on that subject.

Carpenter, Wm. W.—Travels and Adventures in Mexico. New York, 1851. Harper & Brothers.

Catherwood, F.—Views of Ancient Monuments in Central America, Chiapas, and Yucatan. New York, 1844. Bartlett & Welford. A magnificent illustrated work.

Champlain, Samuel.—Narrative of a Voyage to the West Indies and Mexico, in the Years 1599–1602. With maps and illustrations. Hakluyt Society Publication, vol. 23.

Chevalier, M. Michel.—Mexico, Ancient and Modern. London, 1864. John Maxwell & Co. 2 vols. It gives a full account of the Maximilian programme.

Chevalier, Michel.—Mexico before and after the Conquest. Philadelphia, 1826. Carey & Hart.

Chipman, C.—Mineral Resources of Northern Mexico. New York, 1868. Baker & Godwin, printers.

*Church, Geo. E.**—Historical and Political Review of Mexico and its Revolutions.

*Chynowesly.**—The Fall of Maximilian, 1872.

Cincinnatus.*—Travels in the Western Slope of the Mexican Cordillera. San Francisco, 1867.

Clavigero, Francesco Saverio.—History of Mexico. 3 vols. Translated from the Italian by C. Cullen. Philadelphia, 1817. Thomas Dobson.

Cluseret, G.—Mexico and the Solidarity of Nations. New York, 1866. Blackwell, printer.

Cortez, Hernando.—The Dispatches of Hernando Cortez, the Conqueror of Mexico, addressed to the Emperor Charles V.; written during the Conquest, and containing a Narrative of its Events. New York, 1843. Wiley & Putnam.

Dalton, Wm.—Stories of the Conquest of Mexico and Peru. London, 1874. James Blackwood & Co.

Diaz, Bernal.—The Memoirs of the Conquestador Bernal Diaz del Castillo, written by himself, containing a true and full account of the Discovery and Conquest of Mexico and New Spain. 2 vols. London, 1844. J. Hatchard & Son.

Dilworth, W. H.—The History of the Conquest of Mexico, by the celebrated Hernan Cortez. Glasgow, 1785. Printed for the booksellers.

Dunbar, E. E.—The Mexican Papers. New York, 1860. J. A. H. Hasbrouck & Co., printers.

Egloffstein, F. W., Baron.—Contributions to the Geology and the Physical Geography of Mexico. New York, 1864. D. Appleton & Co.

Elton, J. F.—With the French in Mexico. Philadelphia, 1867. J. P. Lippincott & Co.

Evans, A. S.—Our Sister Republic; a gala Trip through tropical Mexico in 1869-1870. Hartford, 1870. Columbian Book Co. Is observations of the author while traveling as one of Hon. W. H. Seward's party.

Farnham, T. J.—Mexico: its Geography, its People, and its Institutions. New York, 1846. H. Long & Brother.

Ferguson's Anecdotical Guide to Mexico. Philadelphia, 1876. Claxton, Remsen & Haffelfinger.

Ferry, Gabriel.—Vagabond Life in Mexico. New York, 1856. Harper & Brothers.

Flint, Henry M.—Mexico under Maximilian. New York, 1867. National Publishing Co. A defense of Maximilian's rule.

Folsom.—Mexico in 1842. New York, 1842. Wiley & Putnam.

Froebel, J.—Seven Years' Travel in Central America, Northern Mexico, and the Far West of the United States. London, 1869. Richard Bentley. This is chiefly on Northern Mexico, and the territory ceded to the United States.

Frost, John.—Pictorial History of Mexico and the Mexican War. Philadelphia, 1848. James A. Bill.

Gage, Thomas.—A New Survey of the West

Indies. A journey of 3,300 miles within the mainland of America. London, 1655. E. Cotes.

Gallatin, Albert.—Notes on the Semi-civilized Nations of Mexico, Yucatan, and Central America. In Transactions of American Ethnological Society, vol. i.

Geiger, John L.—A Peep at Mexico. London, 1874. Trübner & Co. It contains forty-five photographs of places.

Gilliam, Albert M.—Travels over the Table-lands and Cordilleras of Mexico. Philadelphia, 1846. John W. Moore.

Godoy, D.—Things most Remarkable observed by the Spanish at their First Coming to Mexico. In Purchas's Pilgrims, iii., p. 1123 and following.

Gordon, T. F.—The History of Ancient Mexico. 2 vols. Philadelphia, 1832. Published for the author.

Gregory's History of Mexico. Boston, 1847. F. Gleason.

Hall, Basil.—Extracts from a Journal written on the Coasts of Chili, Peru, and Mexico, in the years 1821 and 1822. 2 vols. Edinburgh. Printed by Archibald Constable & Co.

Halls of the Montezumas; or, Mexico in Ancient and Modern Times. New York, 1848. J. C. Burdick.

Hardy, R. W. H.—Travels in the Interior of Mexico in 1825, '26, '27, and '28. London, 1829. Henry Colburn & Richard Bentley.

Haven, Gilbert.—Our Next-Door Neighbor; a Winter in Mexico. New York, 1875. Harper & Brothers.

Helps, Arthur.—The Spanish Conquest in America, and its Relation to the History of Slavery and to the Government of the Colonies. 4 vols. London, 1855–61. J. W. Parker & Son. A portion of this treats of Mexico.

Hill, S. S.—Travels in Peru and Mexico. 2 vols. London, 1860. Longman, Green, Longman & Roberts.

Humboldt, Alex. de (Baron).—Political Essay on New Spain. 4 vols. London, 1822. Longman, Hurst, Rees, Orme & Brown. This is the most elaborate treatise on the resources of the Southwest, or New Spain, that has ever been published. Its review of the products of the precious metals from the conquest to 1804 has been used as a basis for most all subsequent estimates.

Humboldt, Alex. de.—Researches concerning the Institutions and Monuments of the Ancient Inhabitants of America. London, 1814. Longman, Hurst, Rees, Orme & Brown.

Kingsborough (Lord).—Antiquities of Mexico, comprising fac-similes of ancient Mexican paintings and hieroglyphics preserved in the Royal Libraries of Paris, Berlin, and Dresden: in the Imperial Library of Vienna; in the Vatican Library; in the Borgian Museum at Rome; in the Library of the Institute at Bologna; and in the Bodleian Library at Oxford, together with the monuments of New Spain, by M. Dupaix, with their respective scales of measurement and accompanying descriptions. The whole illustrated by many valuable unedited MSS., by Augustine Aglio. In 9 vols. London, 1830. A. Aglia. This is one of the costliest and most magnificent works ever published in the world. Allibone says that the preparation of the first seven volumes cost £32,000 or $160,000.*

Kingsley, Miss.—South by West; or, Winter in the Rocky Mountains, and Spring in Mexico. London, 1874. W. Isbeter & Co.

Kollonitz, Paula (Countess).—The Court of Mexico. London, 1867. Saunders, Otley & Co.

Latrobe, J.—The Rambler in Mexico. New York, 1836. Harper & Brothers.

Lemprière, C.—Notes on Mexico in 1861 and 1862, politically and socially considered. London, 1862. Longman, Green, Longman, Roberts & Green.

Lower California: Its Geography and Character-

---

* See Allibone's "Dictionary of Authors," and "Bibliotheca Americana Nova," by O. Rich, p. 234.

istics, with a sketch of the grant and purposes of the Lower California Company. New York, 1868. M. B. Brown & Co., Printers.

Lyon, G. F.—Journal of a Residence and Tour in the Republic of Mexico in the Year 1826. 2 vols. London, 1828. John Murray.

Lyon, G. F.—The Sketch-Book during Eight Months' Residence in the Republic of Mexico. New York, 1827. J. Dickinson. A collection of curious and interesting pictures.

McSherry, Richard.—El Puchero; or, a Mixed Dish from Mexico. Philadelphia, 1850. Lippincott, Grambo & Co.

Mason, R. H.—Pictures of Life in Mexico. 2 vols. London, 1852. Smith, Elder & Co.

Mayer, Brantz.—Mexico; Aztec, Spanish, and Republican. A historical, geographical, political, statistical, and social account of that country. 2 vols. Hartford, 1852. S. Drake & Co. This is the most elaborate history of Mexico in the English language.

Mayer, Brantz.—Observations on Mexican History and Archæology. Washington, 1856. In Smithsonian Contributions to Knowledge, vol. ix.

Mayer, Brantz.—Mexico as it Was and as it Is. Philadelphia, 1847. G. B. Zieber.

Menonville, M., Nicholas, Joseph Thierry de.—Travels to Guaxaca. In Pinkerton's Voyages, vol. xiii.

Mexico: The Country, History, and People. London, 1863. Published by the Religious Tract Society.

Mexico: A Trip to; or, Recollections of a Ten Months' Ramble. By a Barrister. London, 1851. Smith, Elder & Co.

Mexico: The Modern Traveller. A popular Description, Geographical, Historical and Topographical. 2 vols. Boston, 1830. Wells & Lilly.

Mexico: A Sketch of the Customs and Society during 1824, 1825, and 1826. London, 1828. Longman & Co.

Mill, Nicholas.—History of Mexico. London, 1824. Sherwood, Jones & Co.

Niles, John M.—History of South America and Mexico, * * * to which is annexed a Geographical and Historical View of Texas, by L. T. Pease. 2 vols. Hartford, 1839. H. Huntington, Jr.

Norman, B. M.—Rambles by Land and Water; or, Notes of Travel in Cuba and Mexico. New York, 1845. Paine & Burgess.

Philips, M.—Voyage to Mexico in 1568. In Hakluyt's Voyages, vol. iii., p. 558.

Phillips, John.—Mexico Illustrated in Twenty-six Drawings. London. E. Atchley. A collection of large and magnificent lithographs, illustrating buildings, cities, and scenery in Mexico.

Poinsett, J. R.—Notes on Mexico in the Autumn

of 1822, accompanied by a historical Sketch of the Revolution. Philadelphia, 1824. H. C. Carey & I. Lea.

Prescott, W. H.—History of the Conquest of Mexico, with a Preliminary View of the Ancient American Civilization and the Life of the Conqueror, Hernando Cortez. 3 vols. New York, 1849. Harper & Brothers.

Rankin, Malinda.—Twenty Years among the Mexicans. Cincinnati, 1875. Chase & Hall.

Ranking, John.—Historical Researches on the Conquest of Peru and Mexico, Bogota, Natchez, and Talomeco in the Thirteenth Century, by the Mongols, accompanied with Elephants. London, 1827. Longman, Rees, Orme, Brown & Green. This contains an interesting description of the ancient city of Mexico.

Report of the Committee of Investigation sent in 1873 by the Mexican Government to the Frontier of Texas. New York, 1875. Baker & Godwin, printers.

Robertson, Wm. P.—A Visit to Mexico. 2 vols. London, 1853. Simpkin, Marshall & Co.

Robinson, F.—Mexico and her Military Chieftains, from the Revolution of Hidalgo to the Present Time. Philadelphia, 1847. E. H. Butler & Co.

Robinson, W. D.—Memoirs of the Mexican Revolution. Philadelphia, 1820. Printed for the author.

Ruxton, G. F.—Adventures in Mexico and the Rocky Mountains. New York, 1848. Harper & Brothers.

Salm Salm, F. (Prince.)—My Diary in Mexico in 1861, including the Last Days of the Emperor Maximilian, with Leaves from the Diary of Princess Salm Salm. 2 vols. London, 1868.

Sartorius, C.—Mexico: Landscapes and Popular Sketches. London, 1859. Trübner & Co. Very finely illustrated.

Shepard, A. K.—The Land of the Aztecs; or, Two Years in Mexico. Albany, 1859. Weed, Parsons & Co.

Shufeldt, Robert W., Captain U. S. Navy.—Reports of Explorations and Surveys to ascertain the Practicability of a Ship Canal between the Atlantic and Pacific Oceans by the way of the Isthmus of Tehuantepec. Washington, 1872.

Simon, B. A. (Mrs.)—The Ten Tribes of Israel historically identified with the Aborigines of the Western Hemisphere. London, 1836. R. B. Seeley & W. Burnside. This chiefly on Mexico.

Skinner, J. E. H.—After the Storm; or, Jonathan and his Neighbors in 1865-1866. 2 vols. London, 1866. Richard Bentley. Part of vol. ii. is on Mexico.

Solis, Antonio de.—History of the Conquest of Mexico by the Spaniards. 2 vols. London, 1753.

On page 317 of vol. i. there is a fine view of the ancient Aztec city of Mexico.

Stephens, John L.—Incidents of Travel in Central America, Chiapa, and Yucatan. 2 vols. New York, 1841. Harper & Brothers.

Stephens, John L.—Incidents of Travel in Yucatan. 2 vols. New York, 1843. Harper & Brothers. Illustrated by 120 engravings.

Squier, E. G.—Observations on the Chalchihuitl of Mexico and Central America. New York, 1869.

Stapp, W. P.—The Prisoners of Perote. Philadelphia, 1845. G. B. Zieber & Co.

Taylor, A. S.—Settlement and Exploration of Lower California. In Ross Browne's " Resources of Pacific States."

Tempsky, G. F. von.—Mitla; a Narrative of Incidents and Personal Adventures on a Journey in Mexico, Guatemala, and Salvador. London, 1858. Longman, Brown, Green, Longmans & Roberts.

Thompson, Waddy.—Recollections of Mexico. New York, 1846. Wiley & Putnam.

Tomson, Robert, The Voyage of, to New Spain, in 1555. In Hakluyt's Voyages, vol. iii., p. 531 and following.

Tylor, Edward B.—Anahuac; or, Mexico and the Mexicans, Ancient and Modern. London, 1861. Longman, Green, Longman & Roberts.

Ulloa, Francisco.—Voyage from Acapulco up the

Western Coast of Mexico in 1539. In Hakluyt's Voyages, iii., p. 473.

Vigne, G. T.—Travels in Mexico, South America, etc. London, 1863. 2 vols. W. H. Allen & Co.

Wallace, Lew.—The Fair God; or, The Last of the Tzins. A tale of the conquest of Mexico. Boston, 1873. James R. Osgood & Co.

Ward, H. G.—Mexico in 1827. 2 vols. London, 1828. Henry Colburn. This is an official report to the British Government by the author, who was her Majesty's Chargé d'Affaires in Mexico from 1825–1827. Next to Baron Humboldt's work, it is the most elaborate work on the resources of New Spain in the English language. It treats very fully of the precious metals.

Wilson, R. A.—A New History of the Conquest of Mexico. Philadelphia, 1859. James Challen & Son.

Wilson, R. A.—Mexico and its Religion. New York, 1855. Harper & Brothers.

Young, Philip.—History of Mexico from 1520 to 1847. Cincinnati, 1847. J. A. & U. P. James.

THE AUTHORITIES ON CALIFORNIA.

Allsop, R.*—California and its Gold Mines. 1853. Groombridge.

Bancroft's Tourist's Guide. San Francisco, 1871. A. L. Bancroft & Co.

Binney.*—California Homes for Educated Englishmen. 1875. Simp.

Blake.*—Geological Reconnoissance. New York, 1859.

Borthwick, J. D.—Three Years in California. Edinburgh, 1857. Wm. Blackwood & Sons.

Brace, C. L.—The New West; or, California in 1867-1868. New York, 1869. G. P. Putnam & Son.

Brooks, J. T.—Four Months among the Gold-finders in Alta California. London, 1849. David Bogue.

Bryant, Edwin.—What I saw in California. New York, 1848. D. Appleton & Co.

Buffum, E. G.—Six Months in the Gold Mines. Philadelphia, 1850. Lea & Blanchard.

California: * its Past History, its Present Position. London, 1850.

California and her Gold Regions. (Anon.) Philadelphia, 1849. G. B. Zieber, Agent.

California, * Life in, 1846.—Wiley.

California: * Agricultural Resources. Troy, 1856.

Capron, E. S.—History of California from its Discovery to the Present Time. Boston, 1854. J. P. Jewett & Co.

Chappe de' Auteroche, J.—Voyage to California

to observe the Transit of Venus. London, 1778. Printed for Edward and Charles Dilly.

Colton, Walter.—Three Years in California. New York, 1850. A. S. Barnes & Co.

Cone, Mary.—Two Years in California. Chicago, 1876. S. C. Griggs & Co.

Cronise, T. F.—The Natural Wealth of California. San Francisco, 1868. H. H. Bancroft & Co.

Cutts, J. Madison.—The Conquest of California and New Mexico. Philadelphia, 1847. Carey & Hart.

Delano, A.—Life on the Plains and among the Diggings; an Overland Journey to California. Auburn, 1854. Miller, Orton & Mulligan.

Drake, Sir Francis.—Voyage to California. In Hakluyt's Voyages, iii. 523, etc.

Dunbar, Edward E.—The Romance of the Age; or, The Discovery of Gold in California. New York, 1867. D. Appleton & Co.

Evans, A. S.—A la California; Sketches of Life in the Golden State. San Francisco, 1873. A. L. Bancroft & Co.

Farnham, J. T.—The Early Days of California. Philadelphia, 1862. John E. Potter.

Farnham, J. T.—Life, Adventures, and Travel in California, to which is added the Conquest of California. New York, 1849. Nafis & Cornish.

Farnham, E. W.—California, Indoors and Out. New York, 1856. Dix, Edwards & Co.

Fisher, W. M.—The Californians. New York, 1876. Macmillan & Co.

Foster, G. G.—The Gold Regions of California. New York, 1848. Dewitt & Davenport.

Fremont, J. C.—Geographical Memoir of Upper California. Washington, 1848. Sen. Miscellaneous Doc. 148; 1st sess. 30th Congress.

Fremont and Emory.—Notes of Travel in California. New York, 1849. D. Appleton & Co.

Frost, John.—History of the State of California. Auburn, 1850. Derby & Miller.

Frowd, J. G. P.—Six Months in California. London, 1872. Longman, Green & Co.

Greeley, Horace.—An Overland Journey from New York to San Francisco. New York, 1860. C. M. Caxton, Barker & Co.

Greenhow, R.—History of Oregon and California. Boston, 1844. C. C. Little & James Brown.

Hittell, John S.—The Resources of California, San Francisco, 1874. A. Roman & Co.

Hittell, John S.—Yosemite. Its Wonders, and its Beauties. San Francisco, 1868. H. H. Bancroft & Co. Illustrated with twenty photographs.

Helper, H. R.—The Land of Gold; Reality *vs.* Fiction. New York, 1855. Henry Taylor.

Holmes, Henry A.—Our Knowledge of California and the Northwest Coast one Hundred Years since. Albany, 1870. Joel Munsell.

How to get Rich in California. A History of the Progress and present Condition of the Gold and Silver Mining and other industrial Interests. Philadelphia, 1876. McMorris & Gans. A valuable statistical work.

Huntley, Sir H.—California: its Gold and its Inhabitants. 2 vols. London, 1856. Thomas C. Newby.

Hutchings, J. M.—Scenes of Wonder and Curiosity in California. Illustrated with over one hundred engravings. A Tourist's Guide to the Yosemite Valley. New York, and San Francisco, 1870. A. Roman & Co.

Johnson, T. T.—Sights in the Gold Region. New York, 1850. Baker & Scribner.

Kelley, Wm.—An Excursion to California. London, 1851. 2 vols. Chapman & Hall.

Kneeland, Samuel (Prof.).—The Wonders of the Yosemite Valley, and of California. Boston, 1871. Alexander Moore. It contains excellent photographic views.

Letts, J. M.—California Illustrated. New York, 1852. W. Holdrege. It contains a large number of fine lithographic views.

Lyman, Albert.—Journal of a Voyage to California, and Life in the Gold Diggings. Hartford, 1852. E. T. Pease.

McCollum, W. S.*—California as I saw it. Buffalo, 1850.

Marryat, Frank.—Mountains and Mole-Hills; or, Recollections of a Burnt Journal. New York, 1855, Harper & Brothers.

Nordhoff, Charles.—Northern California, Oregon, and the Sandwich Islands. New York, 1874. Harper & Brothers.

Nordhoff, Charles.—Health, Pleasure, and Residence. New York, 1872. Harper & Brothers. This is one of the best descriptions of California. Is well illustrated.

Norman, Lucia.—A Youth's History of California. San Francisco, 1867. A. Roman & Co.

Notes on California and the Placers. New York, 1850. Harper & Brothers.

Olden, W. R.—A Series of Articles on Southern California. Anaheim, California, 1875.

Palmer, J. W.—The New and the Old; or, California and India in Romantic Aspects. New York, 1859. Rudd & Carleton.

Parkman.—Travels of the Jesuits. 2 vols. London, 1762. Printed for T. Piety. Vol. i. contains an account of the missions of California.

Pioneers, First Annual of. San Francisco, 1877. Printed by W. M. Hinton & Co.

Porquet, F. de.*—California Phrase Book, 1851. Simpkin.

Pioneer.*—4 vols. San Francisco, 1854–1855.

Powell, J. J.—The Golden State and its Resources. San Francisco, 1874. Bacon & Co.

Revere, J. W.—Tour of Duty in California. New York. 1869. C. S. Francis & Co.

Ringold, C.—A Series of Charts, with Sailing Directions, embracing Surveys of Bays and Rivers of California. Washington, 1851.

Robinson, A.—Life in California. New York, 1846. Wiley & Putnam.

Robinson, Fayette.—California and its Gold Regions. New York, 1849. Stringer & Townsend.

Ryan, W. R.—Personal Adventures in Upper and Lower California. 2 vols. London, 1850. Wm. Shoberl.

Saxon, Isabella.—Five Years within the Golden Gate. London, 1868. Chapman & Hall. A description of social life.

Seward, W. H.—Speech in the Senate of the United States on the Admission of California. March 11, 1850. Washington, 1850.

Seyd, Ernest.—California and its Resources. A Work for the Merchant, the Capitalist, and the Emigrant. London, 1858. Trübner & Co.

Shuck, O. T.*—The California Scrap Book. San Francisco, 1869.

Stillman, J. D. B.—Seeking the Golden Fleece. A record of pioneer life in California. To which is annexed Footprints of Early Navigators, other than Spanish, in California. San Francisco, 1877. A. Roman & Co.

Taylor, Wm.—California Life Illustrated. New York, 1858. Published for the author.

Thompson, G. A.*—California and Pacific. 1849. Simpkin.

Thornton, J. Q.—Oregon and California in 1848. New York, 1849. Harper & Brothers.

Todd, J.—The Sunset Land. Boston, 1870. Lee & Shepard.

Truman, B. C.—Semi-tropical California. San Francisco, 1874. A. L. Bancroft & Co.

Turrill, Charles B.—California Notes. San Francisco, 1876. Edward Bosqui & Co., printers.

Tuthill, Franklin.—The History of California. San Francisco, 1866. H. H. Bancroft & Co. It gives a list of the governors under Spain, treats of the Jesuits, Franciscans, land-titles, etc.

Tyson, James L.—Diary of a Physician in California. New York, 1850. D. Appleton & Co.

Tyson, Philip T.—Geology and Industrial Resources of California. Exec. Doc., 1st sess., 31st Congress.

Udell, J.—Incidents of Travel in California. Jefferson, O., 1856. Printed for the author.

Venegas, M.—A Natural and Civil History of

California. 2 vols. London, 1759. Printed for James Rivington.

Weed, Joseph.—A View of California as It is. San Francisco, 1874. Bynon & Wright.

Werth, John J.—A Dissertation on the Resources and Policy of California. Benicia, Cal. St. Clair & Pinkham.

Whitney, J. D.—Geological Survey of California. Printed by authority of the Legislature.

Woods, D. B.—Sixteen Months in the Gold Diggings. New York, 1851. Harper & Brothers.

Wyld, J.*—Guide to the Gold Regions. 1850. Strange.

THE AUTHORITIES ON TEXAS.

Baker, D. W. C.—A Brief History of Texas. New York, 1873. A. S. Barnes & Co.

Baker, D. W. C.—A Texas Scrap-Book, made up of the History, Biography, and Miscellany of Texas and its People. New York, 1875. A. S. Barnes & Co.

Barrow, John.—Facts relating to Northeastern Texas. London, 1849. Simpkin, Marshall & Co.

Bonnell, G. W.—Topographical Description of Texas. Austin, 1840. Clark, Wing & Brown.

Brady, Wm.— Glimpses of Texas. Houston, 1871.

Braman, D. E. E.—Information about Texas. Philadelphia, 1857. J. B. Lippincott & Co.

Cordova, J. D.—Texas, her Resources and her Public Men. Philadelphia, 1858. E. Crozet.

Dewees, W. B.*—Letters from an Early Settler of Texas. Louisville, 1852.

Edwards, D. B.—History of Texas; or, Emigrants', Farmers', and Politicians' Guide. Cincinnati, 1836. J. A. James & Co. It treats of the colonization laws.

Flack, Capt.—The Texan Rifle Hunter; or, Field Sports on the Prairie. London, 1866. John Maxwell & Co.

Foot, H. S.—Texas and the Texans; or, Advance of the Anglo-Americans to the Southwest. Philadelphia, 1841. 2 vols. Thomas Cowperthwaite & Co. It treats of the Spanish colonial policy, Aaron Burr's scheme, etc.

Forney, John W.—What I Saw in Texas. Philadelphia, 1872. Ringwalt & Brown.

Gouge, W. M.—Fiscal History of Texas; its Revenues, Debts, and Currency, 1834–1852. Philadelphia, 1852. Lippincott, Grambo & Co.

Green, T. J.—Journal of the Texian Expedition against Mier. New York, 1845. Harper & Brothers.

Greeley, Horace.—Letters from Texas and the Lower Mississippi. New York, 1871. Tribune Office.

Holley, Mary Austin (Mrs.).—Texas. Lexington, 1836. J. Clarke & Co.

Hooton, Charles.—St. Louis Isle; or, Texiana. London, 1847. Simmons & Ward.

Houston, M. C. (Mrs.).—Texas and the Gulf of Mexico. Philadelphia, 1845. G. B. Zieber.

Ikin, A.*—Texas, 1841. Sherwood.

Jones, A.—Memoranda and Official Correspondence relating to the Republic of Texas; its History and Annexation. New York, 1859. D. Appleton & Co.

Kennedy, Wm.—Texas; its Geography, Natural History, and Topography. New York, 1844. Benjamin & Young.

Kennedy, Wm.—Texas; the Rise, Progress, and Prospects. 2 vols. London, 1841. R. Hastings.

McCalla, W. L.—Adventures in Texas. Philadelphia, 1841. Printed for the author.

Maillard, N. D.—The History of the Republic of Texas, from the Discovery of the Country to the Present Time and the Cause of her Separation from the Republic of Mexico. London, 1842. Smith, Elder & Co.

Montgomery.—Eagle Pass; or, Life on the Border. New York, 1852. G. P. Putnam & Co.

Moore, F.—Description of Texas. New York, 1844. T. R. Tanner.

Morphis, J. M.—History of Texas from its Discovery and Settlement. New York, 1874. United States Publishing Company.

Newell, C.—History of the Revolution in Texas. New York, 1838. Wiley & Putnam.

Olmstead, F. L.—A Journey through Texas. New York, 1857. Dix, Edwards & Co.

Parker, W. B.—Notes taken during the Expedition by Captain R. B. Marcy through Unexplored Texas. Philadelphia, 1856. Hayes & Zell.

Pease, L. T.—Geographical and Historical View of Texas. In appendix of Niles's "History of Mexico."

Prairiedom.—Rambles and Scrambles in Texas. New York, 1845. Paine & Burgess.

Probus.—The Texan Revolution, 1842.

Protest.—The Anti-Texass Legion. Protest of some Freemen, States, and Presses against the Texass Rebellion against the Laws of Nature and of Nations. Albany, 1845. Extremely radical.

Rankin, Melinda.—Texas in 1850. Boston, 1850. Damrell & Moore.

*Smith, E.**—Northeastern Texas, 1849. Hamilton.

Stiff, E.—The Texan Emigrant. Cincinnati, 1840. George Conclin.

Texas.—A Visit to Texas, being the Journal of a Traveller. New York, 1834. Goodrich & Wiley.

*Texas,** A New History of. Cincinnati, 1848.

Texas, History of; or, The Emigrant's Guide to the New Republic. New York, 1845. Nafis & Cornish.

Texas.—An English Question. (Anon.) London, 1837. E. Wilson.

Texas.*—Its Soil and Advantages. E. Wilson, 1848.

Thrall, H. S.—A History of Texas from the Earliest Settlements to the Year 1876. New York, 1876. University Publishing Co.

Western Texas the Australia of America; or, The Place to Live. Cincinnati, 1860.

Woodman, David, Jr.—Guide to Texas Emigrants. Boston, 1835. Printed by M. Hawees.

Yoakum, H.—History of Texas from its First Settlement in 1685 to its Annexation to the United States in 1846. 2 vols. New York, 1855. Redfield. This is the most complete history of Texas yet published.

In addition to the many Spanish records and manuscripts relating to Texas, believed to be in existence in Mexico and Spain, and the above list of works in English, there is an unpublished manuscript by a Swiss scientist and explorer, which probably contains as valuable information about the State of Texas as was ever written. We allude to the Berlandier manuscript, which is more fully described in a subsequent list.

THE AUTHORITIES ON NEW MEXICO.

Albert, J. W.—Report of his Examination of New Mexico in 1846-1847. Washington, 1848. Executive Document 41.

Arny, W. F. M.—Interesting Items regarding New Mexico. Its Agricultural, Mineral, and Pastoral Resources. Santa Fé, 1873. Manderfield & Tucker, printers.

Brevort, Elias.—New Mexico: her Resources and Attractions. Santa Fé, 1874.

Carleton, J. H.—Diary of an Excursion to the Ruins of Abo, etc., in New Mexico. In Smithsonian Report, 1854, p. 296, etc.

Clever, Charles P.—New Mexico: her Resources, etc. Washington, 1868.

Davis, W. W. H.—The Spanish Conquest of New Mexico. Doylestown, Pa., 1869. A thorough, instructive, and highly entertaining work.

Davis, W. W. H.—El Gringo; or, New Mexico and her People. New York, 1857. Harper & Brothers. A description of social life in New Mexico.

Edwards, Frank S.—A Campaign in New Mexico with Colonel Doniphan's Expedition. Philadelphia, 1847. Carey & Hart.

Elkins, S. B.—Speech in the House of Representatives, May 21, 1874, on the Proposed Admission to the Union of New Mexico. In Congressional Record, pp. 295-302.

Espejo, Antonio de, Voyage of, to New Mexico in 1582. In Hakluyt's "Voyages," iii. 464, etc.

Hughes, J. T.—Account of the Conquest of New Mexico. Cincinnati, 1848. In his "Doniphan's Expedition."

McParlin, Thomas A.—Notes on the History and Climate of New Mexico. In Smithsonian Report, 1876.

Meline, James F.—Two Thousand Miles on Horseback; Santa Fé and Back. New York, 1867. Hurd & Houghton. Is chiefly on New Mexico.

Ruffner, Lieutenant.—A Political Problem; New Mexico and the New Mexicans. 1876.

Ruis, Friar Augustin.—Exploration of, to New Mexico in 1581. In Hakluyt's "Voyages," iii., p. 464, etc.

Simpson, J. H.—Report of Exploration and Survey, from Fort Smith, Arkansas, to Santa Fé. House Executive Doc. 45; 1st sess. 31st Congress.

A large portion of the authorities on this Territory will be found in the subsequent list of works too general for the above territorial classification, such as reports of surveys, boundary commissions, etc. Spanish works and records on the history of

New Mexico are very abundant; and when the Territory becomes more developed and populous, those authorities will be sought for, and doubtless translated into English. The recent official report on public libraries, in alluding to the libraries of New Mexico in 1850, says: "The library then contained the manuscript records of the Territory dating back more than three hundred years. This collection of records is probably the oldest in the United States."*

THE AUTHORITIES ON ARIZONA.

Cozzens, S. W.—The Marvellous Country; or, Three Years in Arizona and New Mexico. Boston, 1873. Shepard & Gill.

Hodge, Hiram C.—Arizona as It is; or, The Coming Country. New York, 1877. Hurd & Houghton.

*Johnson, Chas. G.**—History of the Territory of Arizona. San Francisco, 1868.

McCormick, Richard C.—Arizona; its Resources and Prospects. New York, 1865. D. Van Nostrand.

Mowry, Sylvester.—Arizona and Sonora. New

"Public Libraries of the United States." Washington, 1876. See p. 294.

York, 1864. Harper & Brothers. This is chiefly on the mines of Arizona.

Pumpelly, R.—Across America and Asia; Notes of a Five Years' Journey around the World, and of Residence in Arizona, Japan, and China. New York, 1870. Leypoldt & Holt.

Safford, A. P. K.—The Territory of Arizona: a brief History and Summary. Tucson, 1874.

A large portion of the authorities on this Territory, as well as New Mexico, will be found in the subsequent list of works too general for the above territorial classification, such as Government and Pacific Railroad surveys and reports, etc.

Like Texas, New Mexico, and California, it was extensively written up by the Spanish when they were in possession of New Spain, and those works will some time be sufficiently needed to justify translations.

THE AUTHORITIES ON COLORADO.

Blackmore, W.—Colorado and Emigration. London, 1869. Low.

Bowles, S.—Colorado the Switzerland of America. Boston, 1869. Lee & Shepard.

Colorado: Its Resources, Parks, and Prospects, as a new Field for Emigration. London, 1869. Rankin & Co.

Fossett, Frank.—Colorado ; a Historical, Descriptive, and Statistical Work on the Rocky Mountains' Gold and Silver Mining Regions. Denver, 1876.

Greatorex, E.*—Summer Etchings in Colorado. London, 1874.

Pangborn, J. G.—The Rocky Mountain Tourist. Topeka, Kans., 1877. T. J. Anderson. This is chiefly on that portion of New Spain lying within the limits of Colorado which is intersected by the Atchison, Topeka, and Santa Fé Railroad.

Taylor, Bayard. — Colorado ; a Summer Trip. New York, 1867. G. P. Putnam & Son.

Whitney, J. P.—Colorado in the United States of America. London, 1867. Cassell, Petter & Galpin.

Many other authorities on the southern or Spanish portion of Colorado, such as Simpson's account of Coronado's expedition, Hayden's surveys, Wheeler's surveys, etc., etc., will be found in a subsequent list, but are too general for this classification.

THE AUTHORITIES ON NEVADA.

The history of this State is chiefly the history of mines and mining, and very little has been written on the State in separate books.

The annual reports of the United State Commissioner of Mining Statistics, and other works on precious metals, contain the most of the information yet published.

The subject is rich enough to deserve a better supply of authorities. The following is the commencement of its future store of written history:

Powell, J. J.—Nevada ; the Land of Silver. San Francisco, 1876. Bacon & Co.

Quille, Dan de (*Wm. Wright*).—History of the Big Bonanza ; an Authentic Account of the Discovery, History, and Working of the world-renowned Comstock Silver Lode of Nevada. Hartford, 1876. American Publishing Co.

THE AUTHORITIES ON UTAH.

Bonwick, J.—The Mormons and the Silver Mines. London, 1872. Hodder & Stoughton.

Burton, R. F.—The City of the Saints. London, 1861. Longman, Green, Longman & Roberts.

Chandless, Wm.—A Visit to Salt Lake. London, 1857. Smith, Elder & Co.

Codman, John.—The Mormon Country. New York, 1874. United States Publishing Co.

Murphy, J. R.—The Mineral Resources of Utah. San Francisco, 1872. A. L. Bancroft & Co.

Remy and Brenchley.—A Journey to Great Salt Lake. 2 vols. London, 1861. W. Jeffs.

Simpson, J. H.—Explorations across Utah. Washington, 1876.

Stansbury, Howard.—Explorations and Survey of the Valley of the Great Salt Lake of Utah. Philadelphia, 1852. Lippincott, Grambo & Co.

As was stated in the forepart of this chapter, the list of authorities does not embrace pamphlets, legislative documents, works on the Mormon religion, etc. By including the history of the Mormons, this list on Utah could be greatly extended.

AUTHORITIES TOO GENERAL FOR THE ABOVE TERRITORIAL CLASSIFICATION.

The most of the works embraced in this list are official, scientific, business-like, and for business purposes. As a rule they will not be found in the catalogues of public libraries classified with the authorities on the respective States or Territories of the Southwest, for they are too comprehensive and general for such classification. And as the Southwest, or New Spain, is a term unknown to catalogues, it is difficult for the general reader, who is investigating that part of the country, to find all of the authorities. This list is probably not complete, but the author trusts that it is nearly so.

Arispe, Don Miguel Ramos de.—Memorial on the

Natural, Political, and Civil State of the Province of Cohaula in the Kingdoms of Mexico, and those of the new kingdoms of Leon, New Santander, and Texas. Translated from the Spanish. Philadelphia, 1814.

Baldwin, J. D.—Ancient America. New York, 1872. Harper & Brothers.

Bancroft, H. H.—The Native Races of the Pacific States of North America. 5 vols. New York, 1876. D. Appleton & Co. Vol. i. on Wild Tribes. Vol. ii. on Civilized Nations. Vol. iii. on Myths and Languages. Vol. iv. on Antiquities. Vol. v. on Primitive History. This is one of the most elaborate works ever published in the United States; and with the exception of the pages relating to Central America, is chiefly on the native races of the country which constituted New Spain.

Bartlett, J. R.—Personal Narrative of Explorations and Incidents in Texas, New Nexico, California, Sonora, and Chihuahua, connected with the United States and Mexican Boundary Commission during the years 1850, 1851, 1852, 1853. 2 vols. New York, 1854. D. Appleton & Co. Finely illustrated.

Bates, D. B. (Mrs.).—Incidents on Land and Water; or, Four Years on the Pacific Coast. Boston, 1857. Jones, French & Co.

Baxley, H. W.—What I saw on the West Coast

of South and North America. New York, 1865. D. Appleton & Co.

Bell, W. A.—New Tracks in North America. A journal of travel and adventure whilst engaged in the survey for a Southern Railroad to the Pacific Ocean during 1867–1868. 2 vols. London, 1869. Chapman & Hall. Illustrated.

Berlandier, Luis.—The very elaborate work on New Spain, to the preparation of which this author devoted about twenty years' time, has never been published. Judging from the account of it given in the Smithsonian Report for 1854, it must be as elaborate as the works, on the same subject, by Baron Humboldt, and Ward, the British minister. The catalogue alone of these MSS. occupies over two pages of the appendix to the Smithsonian Report above mentioned. The following is a portion of the catalogue there given:

"Travels in Mexico and Texas, 1826 to 1834 inclusive, containing notes upon the statistics, early settlement and Indian tribes between the Sabine and Pacific, etc. 7 vols."

"Travels in Mexico, 1828–1830. Comprising interesting notes of the early settlers of Texas by the Spanish and French; account of the ancient Indian tribes, etc. etc. 3 vols."

"Geography and Statistics of the Republic of Mexico."

"Paintings of thirty different Indian tribes. 1 vol."

"History of the Agriculture of Ancient and Modern Mexico. 1 vol."

"Diary of the Commission of Limits in Northern Mexico, 1830. 3 vols."

In addition to the above, there was a detailed report on the topography, several volumes on meteorology, much in regard to the Indian tribes, and a large number of maps.

According to the report of the Secretary of the Smithsonian Institute, Dr. Berlandier was " a native of Switzerland, and a member of the Academy of Geneva. He came to Mexico in 1826, for the purpose of making a scientific examination of that country. Soon after his arrival he was appointed one of the boundary commission, organized by the then new republic, with the object of defining the boundaries, extent, resources, etc., etc., of the northern or frontier States." * From the time of his arrival in Mexico, until his death in 1851, he was occupied in this detailed examination and review of the Southwest. About the time of his death an officer of the United States army, who was making a scientific exploration of Mexico in the interest of the Smithsonian Institute, learned of the MSS.,

---

* See Smithsonian Report for 1854, pp. 15 and 396-398.

and purchased the same of Dr. Berlandier's widow. He sent the same for safe keeping to the Smithsonian. The portion of the MSS. on meteorology was destroyed by the fire at the Smithsonian in 1865. The rest was withdrawn and sold to some individual. It is to be hoped it will be published and accessible to the public.

Bonnycastle, R. H.—Spanish America; or, A Descriptive, Historical, and Geographical Account of the Dominions of Spain in the Western Hemisphere. Philadelphia, 1819. Abraham Small. This gives the political and territorial divisions and Intendancies.

Bowles, Samuel.—Across the Continent. New York, 1865. Hurd & Houghton.

Box, M. J.—Adventures and Explorations in New and Old Mexico, being the record of ten years of travel and research, and a guide to the mineral treasures of Durango, Chihuahua, the Sierra Nevada (east side), Sinaloa and Sonora (Pacific side), and the Southern part of Arizona. New York, 1869. James Miller.

Browne, J. Ross.—Adventures in the Apache Country. A Tour through Arizona and Sonora, with Notes on the Silver of Nevada. New York, 1869. Harper & Brothers.

Browne, J. Ross.—Resources of the Pacific States. A statistical and descriptive summary. . . .

With a sketch of the settlement and exploration of Lower California. New York, 1869. D. Appleton & Co.

Browne, J. Ross.—Crusoe's Island, California, and Washoe. New York, 1864. Harper & Brothers.

Burney, James.—A Chronological History of Discoveries in the South Sea. 5 vols. London, 1803–1817. Printed by Luke Hansard & Sons.

Butterfield, Carlos.—The United States and Mexican Mail Steamship Line. New York, 1860. J. A. H. Hasbrouck & Co.

Cabeza de Vaca. — The Shipwrecks of Alvar Nunez Cabeza de Vaca. Relation. Washington, 1851. This contains an account of his overland trip through New Mexico and Arizona to meet Cortez' soldiers in Old Mexico.

Carvalho, S. N.—Incidents of Travel and Adventure in the Far West with Colonel Fremont's last Expedition. New York, 1857. Darby & Jackson.

Cassin, John.—Illustrations of Birds of California, Texas, etc. Philadelphia, 1856. J. B. Lippincott & Co.

Champlain, S. de.—Voyage to Mexico, 1599–1602. Translated by A. Wilmere. London, 1859. In Hakluyt's "Voyages," v. 23.

Chilton, J.—Voyage to New Spain, 1568. London, 1810. In Hakluyt's "Voyages," iii. 541, etc.

Coronado, Francisco Vasquez de, The Relation of, in regard to the Country of Cibola in New Mexico, and Arizona. In Hakluyt's "Voyages," iii. 446, etc.

Coulter, J.—Adventures on the West Coast of South America and California. 2 vols. London, 1847.

Cremony, John C.—Life among the Apaches. San Francisco, 1868. A. Roman & Co.

Dana, R. H.—Two Years before the Mast. Boston, 1869. Fields, Osgood & Co.

Domenech, E.—Missionary Adventures in Texas and Mexico. London, 1858. Longman, Brown, Green, Longmans & Roberts.

Domenech, E.—Seven Years' Residence in the Great Deserts of North America 2 vols. London, 1860. Longman, Green, Longman & Roberts. Splendidly illustrated.

Emory, W. H.—Notes of a Military Reconnoissance from Fort Leavenworth, in Missouri, to San Diego, in California. Senate Exec. Doc. No. 7; 1st sess., 30th Congress.

Escalante, Father.—Summary of his Journal of an Expedition in 1776 from Santa Fé to Utah Lake and the Moqui Villages. In appendix of J. H. Simpson's "Explorations Across Utah." Washington, 1872.

Emory, William H.—Report on the United

States and Mexican Boundary Survey. 3 vols. Washington, 1857. Very finely illustrated.

    Vol. I. is descriptive of the country.

    Vol. II. is Report on the Botany.

    Vol. III. is Report on the Zoölogy.

Forbes, Alexander.—California: A History of Upper and Lower California. London, 1839. Smith, Elder & Co.

Graham, Lieut.-Col.—Report on the United States and Mexico Boundary Line. Senate Exec. Doc. No. 121; 32d Congress, 1st sess.

Gray, Asa.—Plantæ Wrightianæ, an Account of a Collection of Plants made by Charles Wright in Texas and New Mexico in 1849. New York, 1852–1853. G. P. Putnam. Also Nos. 22 and 42 of "Smithsonian Contributions."

Gregg, Josiah.—Commerce of the Prairies; or, The Journal of a Santa Fé Trader during Eight Expeditions across the Great Western Prairies, and a Residence of nearly Nine Years in Northern Mexico. 2 vols. New York, 1844. Henry G. Langley. The first volume is chiefly on New Mexico.

Hawks, Henry.—Voyage to New Spain, 1572. In Hakluyt's "Voyages," iii. 549, etc.

Hayden, F. V.—Annual Reports of the United States Geological and Geographical Survey of the Territories to the Department of the Interior. Washington, 1867–1877.

The Seventh Annual Report on the explorations of 1873 contains valuable information in regard to the geology and mining industry of that portion of Colorado lying within the limits of former New Spain.

The Eighth Annual Report on the explorations of 1874 contains reports of the San Juan mines and the ancient ruins in Southwestern Colorado.

The Ninth Annual Report on the explorations of 1875 contains a report on the geology of the San Juan region.

The Tenth Annual Report will contain a further account of the ancient ruins of Southwestern Colorado, New Mexico, and Arizona.

In addition to the annual reports of Prof. Hayden, there is among the miscellaneous publications a "List of Elevations," by Henry Gannett, published in 1877, containing much interesting information about the elevations of the Southwest.

There has also been prepared by this surveying expedition a series of elegant photographs, among which are views of the scenery and ancient ruins of New Mexico, Arizona, and the Spanish portion of Colorado. A collection of these photographs makes an important addition to the authorities on New Spain.

Heap, Gwinn, Harris.—Central Route to the Pacific from the Valley of the Mississippi to California. Illustrated. Philadelphia, 1854. Lippincott, Grambo & Co. This is a route from Missouri through New Spain to Los Angeles.

Hughes, J. T.—Doniphan's Expedition, containing an Account of the Conquest of New Mexico; General Kearney's Overland Expedition to California; Doniphan's Campaign against the Navajos: his unparalleled March upon Chihuahua and Durango; and the Operations of General Price at Santa Fé. Cincinnati, 1848. J. A. & U. P. James.

Ives, J. C.—Report on the Colorado River of the West (36th Cong., 1st sess.; House Exec. Doc. 90). Washington, 1861.

Kendall, G. W.—Narrative of the Texan Santa Fé Expedition. 2 vols. New York, 1850. Harper & Brothers.

Ker, H.—Travels through the Western Interior of the United States, with a particular Description of a great part of Mexico, or New Spain. Elizabethtown, New York, 1816.

Las Casas, Bartholemew de.—An Account of the First Voyages and Discoveries made by the Spanish in America. By Don Bartholemew de las Casas, Bishop of Chiapa. London, 1699.

Macomb, J. N.—Report of the Exploring Expedition from Santa Fé, New Mexico, to the Junction of the Grand and Green Rivers of the great Colorado of the West in 1859. Finely illustrated. Washington, 1876.

McIlvaine, W.—Sketches of Scenery and Notes of Personal Adventure in California and Mexico. Illustrated. Philadelphia, 1850.

Marcy, R. B.—Thirty Years of Army Life on the Border. London, 1866. Sampson Low, Son & Marston.

Niza, Marco de.—A Relation touching his Discovery of Cenola, or Cibola, in New Mexico and Arizona. In Hakluyt's Voyages, vol. iii., 438, etc.

Pacific Railroad.—Reports of Explorations and Surveys to ascertain the most practicable and economical Route for a Railroad from the Mississippi River to the Pacific Ocean, made under the direction of the Secretary of War. 12 vols. Washington, 1855–1860. The following is not a complete table of contents of these twelve volumes, but an index to portions of interest in the investigation of the resources of the Southwest :

Vol. I. contains a report by the Secretary of War reviewing the various reports submitted to him, and routes explored.

Vol. II. contains a finely illustrated report by Lieutenant E. G. Beckwith on explorations near the 38th and 39th parallels. Also another report by Lieutenant Beckwith on explorations near the 41st parallel. A report by Captain John Pope on explorations near the 32d parallel from the Red River to the Rio Grande. An illustrated report by John Torrey and Asa Gray on the botany along the 32d parallel. A report by Wm. P. Blake on the geology near the 32d parallel. A report by Lieutenant John G. Parke on explorations for that portion of the 32d parallel route lying between Dona Ana, on the Rio Grande, and the Pima villages, on the Gila River. An extract from a report by Lieutenant-Colonel Emory on the region near the 32d parallel.

Vols. III. and IV. contain a report, in six parts, by Lieutenant A. W. Whipple, assisted by Lieutenant J. C. Ives, on explorations near the 35th parallel. Part I. is a finely illustrated description of the journey. It contains a description of Zuni, or the former city of Cibola. Part II. is on the topographical features of the route. Part III. is on Indian tribes. Part IV. is on the geology. Part V. is on the botany of the route.

Vol. V. contains a report, in four parts, by Lieutenant R. S. Williamson, on explorations in California for railroad routes to connect with those near the 32d and 35th parallels. Part I. is a finely illustrated description of the country. Part II. is an illustrated report on geology by W. P. Blake. Part III. is on botany.

Vol. VII. contains a report, in three parts, by

Lieutenant John G. Park, on explorations from San Francisco Bay to Los Angeles, and from the Pimas villages, on the Gila River, to the Rio Grande near the 32d parallel. Part I. is a general report descriptive of the country and finely illustrated. Part II. is a report on the geology of the route. Part III. is on botany.

Vol. XI. contains a review of the various explorations from 1800 to 1857, such as the explorations of Lewis and Clarke, Bonneville, Simpson, Fremont, and many others. It also contains maps, profiles, and elaborate sketches illustrating the contents of preceding volumes.

Palmer, Wm. J.—Report of Surveys across the Continent, in 1867-8, for a Route extending the Kansas Pacific Railway to the Pacific Ocean at San Francisco and San Diego. Philadelphia, 1869. W. B. Selheimer, printer.

Pike, Z. M., Capt. United States Army.—Diary of a Tour through the Interior Provinces of New Spain in the year 1807, under an escort of Spanish dragoons.

Powell, J. W.—Exploration of the Colorado River of the West. Washington, 1875. Finely illustrated.

Ramusius, M. John Baptista.—A Brief Discourse concerning the Three Voyages of Marco de Niza, Coronado, and Alarchon. In Hakluyt's Voyages, iii., p. 434, etc.

Rusling, James F.—The Great West and the Pacific Coast. New York, 1877. Sheldon & Co. A part of this is on Arizona and Southern California.

Ryan, W. R.—Personal Adventures in Upper and Lower California. 2 vols. London, 1850. Wm. Shoberl.

Schaeffer, L. M.—Sketches of Travel in South America, Mexico, and California. New York, 1860. James Egbert, printer.

Shepard, A. K.—Papers on Spanish America. Albany, 1868. Joel Munsell.

Simpson, J. H.—Coronado's March in search of the "Seven Cities of Cibola," and a Discussion of their probable Location. In "Smithsonian Report," 1869. This is as interesting as a novel.

Simpson, J. H.—Journal of a Military Reconnoisance from Santa Fé to the Navajo Country. Philadelphia, 1852. Lippincott Grambo & Co. Is finely illustrated.

Sitgreaves, L.—Report of an Expedition down the Zuni and Colorado Rivers. Washington, 1853. Profusely illustrated. Sen. Exec. Doc. 59; 2d sess., 32d Cong.

Spanish Settlements in America, An account of. Edinburgh, 1762.

Squier, E. G.—New Mexico and California. The Ancient Monuments, etc. In "American Review," November, 1848.

Taylor, Bayard.—Eldorado ; or Adventures in the Path of Empire. New York, 1854. G. P. Putnam.

Wheeler, G. M., Lieutenant.—Reports upon the Geographical and Geological Explorations and Surveys West of the 100th Meridian. 7 vols. Washington, 1875.

These explorations are under the control of the War Department. Only volumes three and five, and part of volume four are yet published. But as the other volumes will soon appear, and as these Reports are among the most interesting and valuable of the "Authorities" on the Southwest, we will place all of the volumes in this list.

Vol. I. will contain a Geographical Report.

Vol. II. will contain a Report on Astronomy and Meteorology.

Vol. III. contains a Report on Geology and Mineralogy.

Vol. IV. contains a Report on Paleontology.

Vol. V. contains a Report on Zoölogy.

Vol. VI. will contain a report on Botany.

Vol. VII. will contain a Report on Ethnology, Philology, and Ruins.

In addition to the Reports a valuable collection of large photographs of scenery and ruins in New Mexico and Arizona have been taken.

Wise, Lieutenant.—Los Gringos ; or, An Inside

View of Mexico and California, etc. New York, 1849. Baker & Scribner.

Wislizenus, A.—Memoir of a Tour to Northern Mexico, connected with Colonel Doniphan's Expedition. Washington, 1848. (Sen. Doc. No. 26; 1st sess., 30th Cong.) This report contains much information about New Mexico.

Wright, John A.—A paper on the Character and Promise of the Country on the Southern Border along or near the 32d Parallel. Philadelphia, 1876. Review Printing House.

RÉSUMÉ.

The above list of English authorities embraces one hundred and six on Mexico, eighty-three on California, forty-six on Texas, sixteen on New Mexico, eight on Arizona, eight on Colorado, two on Nevada, eight on Utah, and sixty-four too general for the above classifications, making a total of three hundred and forty-one. Yet the Southwest is a country comparatively new to Anglo-American civilization. Why then so many works in English? It is because the subject is rich in attractive material for the historian. Not only does the Aztec civilization and the Spanish conquest furnish a mint of remarkable and brilliant events and facts, as attractive as romance, but the solid basis of wealth furnishes the writer on material subjects with an abundance of interesting facts.

It will be noticed that a large portion of the list on Mexico, particularly the works on the resources, were published in London. It is, as will appear in a subsequent chapter, because of their extensive commerce with Mexico, and large investments in mines, that the English people have so carefully examined and thoroughly reviewed the wealth of that portion of the Southwest.

A noticeable feature of the books on the Aztec history is the enthusiasm of the writers, which the critic is sometimes disposed to call exaggeration. From the time Cortez sent his glowing dispatches to the King of Spain, and Diaz, the historian of the achievements of Cortez's army, described the splendors and luxuries of the Aztec capital, to the time that Prescott wrote his fascinating history of the Conquest, the same spirit of enthusiasm and admiration crops out in the writings of most of the historians. The critics who doubt the truthfulness of these histories cannot do better than consider the facts and figures in regard to the wealth of ancient Mexico, or visit some public library, which is so fortunate as to possess a set of Lord Kingsborough's massive volumes or the antiquities, and see for themselves the fac-similes of the picture-writings, and the illustrations of the ancient temples and other ruins.

But quite as noticeable is the enthusiastic spirit

of admiration which appears so frequently in the books of modern writers who are dealing with the resources of New Spain instead of its classic history. The leading writers on the resources, those who have examined New Spain carefully, and in a business-like manner, seem to be surprised at the result of their investigation. As an illustration of this tendency on the part of prominent writers, which one frequently meets with in the examination of the various authorities, we will quote the tributes of three authors, each one on a different portion of New Spain, viz.: Mexico, California, and Texas. Lempriere in his " Notes on Mexico," published in London, in 1862, says: "The merciful hand of Providence has bestowed on the Mexicans a magnificent land abounding in resources of all kinds—a land where none ought to be poor, and where misery ought to be unknown—a land whose products and riches of every kind are abundant, and as varied as they are rich. It is a country endowed to profusion with every gift that man can desire or envy; all the metals from gold to lead; every sort of climate from perpetual snow to tropical heat, and inconceivable fertility." . . . "One thing alone is wanting, that is a government." *

---

* "Notes on Mexico," by Lempriere. See introduction to his book.

Ernest Seyd, whose reputation for ability as a writer on finance gives weight to his opinions, made a careful examination of the resources of California, and in the introduction to his chapter on its agriculture, said: " We will begin by making the following assertion. *There does not exist under the sun a country so wonderfully endowed with agricultural advantages as California, not a country more brilliant in its climate, nor one whose soil is more productive.*" * The italics are his.

Of another portion of New Spain, Horace Greeley wrote in 1872; " Texas is as large as France, with a more genial climate and far richer soil. She has to-day less than one million inhabitants, while France (as reduced by the late war) has more than thirty-six millions. She has more and better timber, and more cattle and horses than France. Why should not her fortieth part of France's population be rapidly increased to a twentieth, a tenth, and before the close of this century to a fifth or fourth? Why should not this State be the home of ten millions of the human family early the next century?" †

If the future development of the Southwest is in accordance with its wealth, and possibilities, and the expectation of those who have most carefully

---

* " California and its Resources," London, 1858, p. 114.
† Greeley's Letters from Texas, p. 29-30.

studied its past record, and its resources, we may expect a degree of civilization and luxury which will develop sufficient material for future histories and reviews far more numerous and entertaining than the authorities thus far written.

CHAPTER VI.

THE FOREIGN COMMERCE OF MEXICO.

ITS NATURAL COURSE.

No intention of nature is more clearly indicated than that the commercial exchanges between Mexico and the outside world should be chiefly with the United States. Baron Humboldt has called attention to the great highway extending along the table-lands from Northern New Mexico to Southern Old Mexico, as one of the wonders of nature. In a previous chapter we have reviewed the topographical features, showing how the general course of the plateaus is northwardly through Mexico into the United States, and how the peculiar formation makes an almost insurmountable barrier between the coasts and great interior of Mexico. The commercial significance of this natural formation was officially and very clearly shown a few years ago in the report of the Mexican Committee on Mining Taxes, as follows: "The central table-land of our country is separated from either sea-coast by rugged mountains and deep ravines breaking it into longitudinal zones of different temperatures and varied productions; but this fact almost cuts off communication between these zones and the sea-coast east or west. While such natural difficulties exist, increased by territorial extent, manufactures and agriculture cannot thrive, because the cost of transportation is so great, we cannot contend with foreign competition, and our vegetable products must be confined to home consumption."* In a history of the Mexican Railway, published at Mexico during the past year, we find still further testimony in regard to the barriers nature has placed in the way of commerce between the coasts and table-lands, viz., "the ascent from the coast to the central table-lands is difficult. Large masses of rock require to be perforated, lofty summits have to be overcome, behind which the fertile plains and valleys of the center open out to a great extent." †

Comparatively speaking Mexico is without a river-system, hence transportation must be by land instead of water. The table-lands, running northwardly, furnish excellent facilities, and, in fact, almost the only facilities for commercial highways.

Again, nature's intention in regard to the course

---

* See Appendix to Blake's "Production of Precious Metals," p. 318.
† History of Mexican Railway by Baz and Gallo, p. 13.

of trade appears in the character of the products. Mexico produces necessities and luxuries which the United States cannot produce, and we in turn produce much that Mexico needs and does not produce or manufacture.

We would then naturally expect an extensive intercourse and commerce between these two great and adjoining republics. Are the intentions of nature observed in this respect?

MEXICO'S EXCHANGES WITH ALL COUNTRIES.

At the time Baron Humboldt wrote, the port of Vera Cruz was the only one frequented for the purposes of foreign trade, hence the statistics given may be said to represent all the exports and imports. For the year 1802 the total exports, via Vera Cruz, were $38,447,367; and the total imports, $21,998,588. Of the above total of exports about three-fourths, or $29,247,529, was silver coined and wrought.

For the year 1803, the total exports, via Vera Cruz, were $14,482,917; and the total imports, $19,866,717. Of the exports for this year, silver constituted considerably over half, or $9,190,676.*

At that time most of the foreign exchanges of Mexico were with Europe, and Humboldt, in order to give a fair illustration, or average, of the value

---

* See Humboldt's "New Spain," p. 37–39.

to Europe of Spanish-American trade, tells how he formed his estimates, viz.: "To know as nearly as possible the value of the importations of Spanish-America, I endeavored to inform myself on the spot in each province of the state of commerce of the principal ports. I procured information relative to the goods registered and those which were smuggled, and I turned, in a particular manner, my attention to those years when, either from a free trade with *neutrals*, or from the sales of *prizes*, a province was glutted with European and East India commodities."* From the statistics which he gives on this subject we have selected those which relate to Mexico. It will be observed, however, that the statistics of Guatemala are combined with those of Mexico, but, as the chief part belongs to Mexico, the reader can form a pretty correct idea of the value of that trade between Mexico and Europe:

	Imports from Europe and Asia, including Contraband.	Exports.	
		Agricultural Produce.	*Produce of Silver and Gold.*
Viceroyalty of New Spain and Capitania General of Guatemala.	$22,000,000	$9,000,000	$22,500,000

Ward gives as the foreign commerce of the whole of Mexico for the period of twenty-five years.

---

* Idem, p. 126, 127.

1796–1820, the exports and imports of the port of Vera Cruz, viz.: *

Exports.	Dollars.
Precious metals	209,777,206
American produce	69,757,017
Total	279,534,223

Imports.	Dollars.
European productions	224,447,132
American productions	34,658,808
Total	259,105,940

He gives the annual average of that period as follows:

Exports.	Dollars.
Precious metals	8,391,088
Other produce	2,790,280
Total	11,181,368

Imports.	Dollars.
European manufactures and produce	8,977,885
American produce	1,386,352
Total	10,364,237

* Ward's Mexico, i. 413–417.

It will be observed that this annual average for the whole period is much less than that at the commencement of the present century as given by Humboldt. The decrease was caused by political troubles in Mexico arising from the attempt at independence in 1810, which continued until the independence was established in 1821. In the same manner, and for the same reason, did the products of silver and gold decrease after 1810, as we have shown in a previous chapter.

The foreign commerce of Mexico had, prior to the war with the United States, which commenced in 1846, recovered from the depressing effects of her revolutionary struggle. To illustrate the extent of her foreign trade at that period, Mayer, in his history of Mexico, took the year 1844 as a fair illustration. He gives the statistics as follows : *

    Total exports............... $11,032,835
    Total imports............... 21,139,234

Of the total exports, nearly all, or $10,932,416, was precious metals, and precious metals in Mexico may be called silver.

A few years after the war with the United States, the foreign commerce of Mexico had increased several millions in value. According to the " States-

---

* Mayer's History of Mexico, ii. 99-100.

man's Year Book," the trade of 1856 was as follows:

  Total exports.................. $28,000,000
  Total imports.................. 26,000,000

And for the ten years 1859–1868, the same authority gives the annual average of total exports and imports as follows, viz.:

  Exports..................... $27,000,000
  Imports 24,000,000

The above totals are inclusive of precious metals as well as products and manufactures.

The total exports and imports of the year 1870 were as follows:

  Exports..................... $24,135,000
  Imports 23,478,000

and of the exports of that year, $17,210,000 was silver.

We have been unable to find the statistics of the total foreign trade of Mexico for every year, so instead of giving a complete table of statistics, we can only take certain years or periods. To illustrate the amount and nature of that trade at the present time, we will take the statistics for the year ending June 30, 1873, as given in the annual report of the State Department on the Commercial Relations. That authority gives the totals as follows: *

> Exports $33,168,609
> Imports 29,062,406

and of that total of exports, over three-fourths, or $25,373,673, was precious and other metals, of which it is safe to say nearly all was silver. Over one-third, or $10,531,970, of the imports of that year was "cotton stuffs," and it is safe to say almost all of that item of imports was from distant Europe, instead of the great cotton-producing State of Texas just across the boundary line. To show what markets Mexico patronizes, we take from the same authority the following table of imports and exports by countries for the same year ending June 30, 1873: †

Countries.	Imports.	Exports.
Miscellaneous..................	....	$1,477,458 57
Italy.......................	$9,035 22....	17,389 00
Great Britain................	10,180,589 37....	12,479,547 57
United States................	7,420,419 43....	11,366,530 76
France......................	4,817,110 63....	4,604,417 38
New Granada (via Panama)....	1,233,429 53....	1,579,015 12
Spain and Cuba...............	1,394,211 53....	752,891 91
Germany.....................	3,890,496 17....	802,643 83
Central America (Guatemala, and Honduras)...........	105,479 32....	80,999 52

---

* See Commercial Relations for 1875, p. 1129.
† Idem, p. 1129.

Ecuador	$10,430 39	$2,931 75
China	825 25	
Belgium	380 10	4,784 00
Total	$29,062,406 94	$33,168,609 41

It will be observed, from this statement, that Mexico purchases chiefly in the European market. Omitting the imports from Spain, because the statistics are combined with those of Cuba, the total purchases from Europe amount to $18,897,611, as against $7,420,419 from the United States.

On the Pacific coast of Mexico, the European monopoly is still more noticeable. Of the foreign commerce of that coast, the United States consul at Guaymas reported to the State Department in 1873: "It is almost entirely in the hands of the Germans, Spanish, and English. In this port leading merchants are Mexicans and Spanish. No American importing house on the West coast, and only one commission house of any importance which is in Guaymas."*

MEXICO'S EXCHANGES WITH THE UNITED STATES.

The annual reports of the United States on commerce and navigation commence with the year ending September 30, 1821, the same year that Mexico

---

* Commercial Relations for 1873, p. 825.

became an independent republic. But in the statistical view of the commerce of that year, Mexico is not mentioned, nor is the trade with Mexico given separately until the year ending September 30, 1825. Taking the statistics for 1825 and 1830, and every tenth year thereafter, as given in those official reports, we have the following view of the exchanges between the two republics. The statistics are inclusive of specie and bullion as well as produce and manufactures:

Year Ending	Total Exports to Mexico.	Total Imports from Mexico.
Sept. 30, 1825	$6,470,144	$4,044,647
" 1830	4,837,458	5,235,241
" 1840	2,515,341	4,175,001
June 30, 1850	2,012,827	2,135,366
" 1860	5,354,073	6,935,872
" 1870*	5,875,396	13,099,031

The statistics given by the Bureau of Statistics are for the past three years, as follows: †

Year Ending	Total Exports to Mexico.	Total Imports from Mexico.
June 30, 1874	$6,004,370	$13,239,905
" 1875	5,770,783	11,634,983
" 1876	6,208,172	12,505,753

* The statistics of this year are from "Quarterly Report of Bureau of Statistics," No. 1, p. 93.
† Idem, p. 93.

It will be observed that the United States exports less to Mexico at the present time than she did fifty-one years ago, when Mexico had just commenced as an independent republic. On the other hand, the imports from Mexico are three times as large as in 1825.

As Mexico and the United States are adjoining American republics, the natural inference to be derived from the above statistics is that we do not produce nor manufacture what Mexico needs; and that Mexico cannot supply products in demand here. But the facts prove that inference is incorrectly drawn. What, then, are the facts?

Of the $10,531,970 worth of cotton stuffs purchased by Mexico during the year, from June 30, 1872, to June 30, 1873, the United States supplied from her own products and manufacture only the following insignificant amount in value, viz.: *

Unmanufactured cotton	$74,352
Manufactured cotton (colored)	66,185
" " (uncolored)	155,657
All other cotton stuffs	73,244
Total value	$369,438

Yet the United States can successfully and pro-

---

* See Annual Report on Commerce and Navigation by Bureau of Statistics.

fitably compete with every nation on earth in both the production and manufacture of cotton.

Not only were cotton stuffs the chief item of Mexico's purchases for the above-mentioned year, but they have constituted the chief item of her imports every other year of the present generation. It follows, then, that there is some other than a natural barrier to our supplying her chief demand.

Quicksilver is another item of Mexico's imports, her purchases of that commodity, in 1873, being in value $2,184,014.* Yet but a small portion of it was purchased from the United States, notwithstanding the fact that the part of this country where it is produced in great profusion is the portion nearest to Mexico.

We have already observed that coffee and sugar are products peculiarly adapted to the soil and climate of Mexico. Our demand for those products is so great that the United States imports each year over fifty million dollars' worth of coffee; and during the last three years the annual average value of our imports of sugar and molasses has been upward of eighty-one million dollars.† Yet Mexico supplies but a small fraction of this demand.

As we stated in the outset, this is a book of facts

---

* See Paper on Mexico in Annual Cyclopædia for 1876.
† See Quarterly Report, No. 1, of Bureau of Statistics, p. 97.

—not theories—so we will not discuss principles of political economy. But, as a matter of fact, it is safe to assert that whatever theory of political economy is responsible for the above showing, needs to be remodeled.

CHAPTER VII.

THE ADVANCE OF RAILWAYS.

THE IMPORTANCE OF NATIONAL HIGHWAYS.

IN the palmy days of the Roman Empire, good public highways were considered indispensable to the welfare of the State. Gibbon, in describing its magnificent system of military roads, says: "No country was considered subdued till it had been rendered pervious to the arms and authority of the conqueror."* The victories of peace, as well as war, require the same aids for their advancement. At the present stage of civilization, the nation which neglects to supply its territory with suitable roads will be slow in its material development, and will fall behind in the race for commercial supremacy. New Spain is no exception to this fundamental rule. Nor is the United States an exception in competition with other nations for the trade of Mexico. Even the early native races of New Spain, and other parts of Spanish America, recog-

---

* Gibbon's Rome, i. 63.

nized this fundamental principle and acted upon it. Long before the Spanish had discovered Peru, the native races had completed a costly system of internal improvements by building highways for their armies and commerce. Bancroft says: "Among the most remarkable Peruvian remains are the paved roads which cross the country in every direction especially from north to south. Two of the grandest highways extended from the region north of Quito, southwest to Cuzco, and, according to some authors, still farther to Chili. One runs over the mountains, the other chiefly through the plains. Their length is at least twelve hundred miles, and the grading of the mountain-roads presented, as Mr. Baldwin believes, far greater difficulties than the Pacific Railroad. These roads are from eighteen to twenty-six feet wide, protected at the sides by a thick wall, and paved generally with stone-blocks, but sometimes with a mixture of cement and fine stone, an aboriginal infringement on the Macadam process. The highways followed a straight course and turned aside for no obstacle. Ravines and marshes were filled up with masonry, and the solid rock of the mountains was cut away for many miles." *

The same historian of the native races says of a

---

* Bancroft's "Native Races," iv. 794-5.

road in Yucatan, one of the Southern States of New Spain, " M. Charnay found a magnificent road from seven to eight mètres wide, whose foundation is of immense stones surmounted by a concrete, perfectly preserved, which is covered with a coating of cement two inches thick. This road is everywhere about a mètre and a half above the surface of the ground." *

These accounts, from ancient history, of costly highways, are a better indication of a high degree of civilization and prosperity of the classic nations than are the stories of their ancient temples and ruins. They show that the Romans, the Incas of Peru, and the Aztecs of Mexico had already adopted theories of government, had advanced beyond the recluse state, to intercourse among themselves and neighboring nations, to a desire for civilization and commerce.

The far-seeing father of the Republic of the United States did not overlook the importance of national highways. After he had exchanged the duties of the soldier for those of the statesman, he became an earnest advocate of a system of internal improvements to connect the Atlantic States with the Mississippi Valley. His letters in 1784, and 1785, to the President of Congress, and to the Gov-

---

* Idem, p. 266–267.

ernor of Virginia, show that he considered it important for political, as well as ccmmercial reasons, that the waters of the Potomac or James River should be connected with those of the Ohio by means of a canal. That in this way would the settlers in the Mississippi Valley be bound to the Atlantic States by ties of interest, and the danger of their uniting their fortunes with the foreign nations in the rear be thereby averted.*

But the civilization of the present day demands a *particular class* of highways. Civilization, and railways, and commerce, go hand in hand, and each helps the other. The advance of the material development of any country intersected by railways is as much faster than formerly, as is the speed of the locomotive greater than the old-fashioned stage coach. The recent official report on the internal commerce of the United States says that, "during the year 1876, eighty-three per cent. of all the grain receipts of the Atlantic seaports was by rail, and it is estimated that over ninety per cent. of all the commerce between the West and the seaboard is now carried on over the great trunk railroads." † So important is this particular class of highways, in the exchanges of the present day,

---

* The Writings of George Washington, ix. 58–119.
† First Annual Report on the Internal Commerce of the United States, by Joseph Nimmo, Washington, 1877, p. 8.

that over three-fourths of the commerce of St. Louis, the central city of the finest river system of the whole world, was, during the year 1875, carried by rail; or to be exact, seventy-eight per cent. was by rail, and twenty-two per cent. by river.* It seems odd, in this material age, to be talking of the importance of railways; but it also appears strange that the great Southwest, the richest portion of the earth in precious metals, and the oldest part of America in European civilization, is comparatively a stranger to railways, and is permitting its riches to remain undeveloped. What are the facts and figures?

THE ADVANCE OF RAILWAYS IN THE UNITED STATES AND THE SOUTHWEST.

The second half of the first century of the republic witnessed the commencement of the first railway in this country. It was in New England instead of New Spain, and near Boston. But it was simply a freight line, of a few miles, to bring to market the products of a stone quarry.† The first railway proper, as described by Poor, was commenced " on the fourth of July, 1828, the first act

---

* Idem, p. 107.
† Manual of Railways of the United States, 1876-77, by H. V. Poor, p. v.

being performed by the venerable Charles Carroll of Carrollton, the only surviving signer of the Declaration of Independence. At the close of the ceremony of breaking ground, Mr. Carroll said, "I consider this among the most important acts of my life, second only to that of signing the Declaration of Independence, if even second to that." * This was the beginning of the present Baltimore and Ohio road. Ever since then railways have been gradually advancing westward; in the meanwhile they have been intersecting every portion of the Eastern States. Not until the third quarter of the first century did they cross the Mississippi River; and not until 1850 did they enter the limits of New Spain. A glance at the map in the forepart of this volume, shows that they have not yet crossed the great interior of New Spain, but end abruptly near the borders, as if afraid to trespass upon a country so rich in treasures.

The following table shows the mileage of railways of the United States, New Spain, and the Mexican half of New Spain at the close of periods of five years beginning with 1830, and ending with the close of 1875, or the close of the first century.†

---

* Idem, p. v.

† Nearly all of the following statistics are compiled from Poor's "Railway Manual," for 1876-77 and 1877-78.

	United States.	New Spain.	Mexico.
1830	41	0	0
1835	1,098	0	0
1840	2,818	0	0
1845	4,633	0	0
1850	9,021	7	7
1855	18,374	58	10
1860	30,635	350	20
1865	35,085	767	88
1870	52,906	2,992	217
1875	74,658	5,069	327

The next table shows the mileage of railways of the various portions of New Spain at the end of periods of five years each commencing with 1850, and ending with the close of 1875.

Year.	Mexico.	California.	Texas.	Utah.	Nevada.	S. & W. Colorado.	New Mexico.	Arizona.	Corner of Wyoming.
1850	7	0	0	0	0	0	0	0	0
1855	10	8	40	0	0	0	0	0	0
1860	20	23	307	0	0	0	0	0	0
1865	88	214	465	0	0	0	0	0	0
1870	217	925	711	257	593	0	0	0	289
1875	327	1,503	1,685	515	650	100	0	0	289

From the above tables it appears that the United States had 9,021 miles of railway when New Spain had but 7 miles; that the portion of the United States which was acquired from Mexico had but 48 miles, when the rest of the United States had

18,326 miles; that, with the exception of 767 miles, all the railways of the Southwest were built during the last ten years of the first century of the republic; *that at the present time there is not a single mile of railway in any of those rich border States— New Mexico, Arizona, Chihuahua, Sonora, and Durango; that there is not a single mile of railway connecting the two great wealthy and neighboring republics*, the one composed of thirty-eight States, nine Territories, and a federal District, the other composed of twenty-seven States, one Territory, and a federal District.

THE ADVANCE OF RAILWAYS IN THE SOUTHWEST COMPARED WITH THAT OF OTHER COUNTRIES AND THE WORLD.

We have on a previous page claimed that the United States has at her own door a more magnificent land than India, awaiting an adequate development of its riches. It may be interesting, for purposes of comparison, to see what steps the English people have taken to develop the resources of their distant possession. When Lord Dalhousie was Governor-General of India he planned a system of railways which have been constructed to the extent of 7,152 miles.* Lines of road start from the

---

* "History of India," by L. J. Trotter, p. 348, and Poor's "Railway Manual" for 1877–78, p. xlix.

two great harbors of India, one on the east and the other on the west coast, and extend into, diverge, and intersect the great interior, forming a network of railways which makes possible a suitable development of that rich country. The Statesman's Year Book, for 1877, says: " The internal commerce of India has been vastly developed of late years by the construction of several great lines of railways made under the guarantee of the Government. In the year 1845 two great private associations were formed for the purpose of constructing lines of railroad in India; but the projectors found it impossible to raise the necessary funds for their proposed schemes without the assistance of the State. It was therefore determined by the Indian Government to guarantee to the railway companies, for a term of 99 years, a rate of interest of 5 per cent. upon the capital subscribed for their undertakings." *

But the English people were not content with the development of their own India. Their enterprise seeks also the riches of Mexico, and English capitalists have completed, and are the chief owners of the railway from Vera Cruz, the most important harbor of the republic, to the highly elevated Capital. As this line constitutes nearly all of the railway mileage of Mexico, Englishmen may be said to

---

* " Statesman's Year Book " for 1877, p. 696.

monopolize the most important of the internal improvements of that rich land. Their commercial policy is more noticeable when we consider that they came to a distant American republic to construct a commercial highway which, on account of the topographical obstacles, is one of the most remarkable achievements of railway engineering. A recent work on Mexico, published in London, says: "The line may be divided into three sections; the first from Mexico over the plateau of *Tierra Fria* to *Boca del Monte*, a distance of 156 miles; thence down the steep descent of the *Cumbres* to *Paso del Macho*, 60 miles; and finally thence along the gently sloping *Tierra Caliente* to Vera Cruz, 47 miles." Of the middle section of the line the author says: "In a distance of 25 miles, the road descends almost 4,000 feet, where curves of 300 feet radius, and gradients of three or four per cent., often over loose and yielding ground, follow one another in quick succession." *

Comparing different portions of Spanish America, we find that Pizzaro's Peru has nearly three times as much railway mileage as Cortez's Mexico.

At the commencement of 1877, Peru had 1,238 miles already built. At the present time there is in process of construction a line which had been

---

* "Peep at Mexico" by J. L. Geiger, pp. 326 and 327.

appropriately termed "a railway in the clouds," * extending from the Pacific Ocean, across the Andes, at a height above the sea of 15,645 feet, to the waters of the Amazon River on the east. The line is to be continued eastward until it unlocks the treasures of the Cerro de Pasco silver mines.

The Argentine Republic, another portion of Spanish America, and, as usual with Spanish American countries, rich in silver, has now 1,466 miles of railway. That Government, in 1863, guaranteed to Mr. Wheelwright, a native of New England, the interest on a certain sum per mile to enable him to build the Grand Central Argentine Railway. At the inauguration of the work, the President of the republic said: "Every one must rejoice on the opening of this great road, for it will tend to people solitudes, to give riches where there is poverty, and to institute order where anarchy reigns." †

These facts indicate that the Spanish nations of South America are entering upon a new era of development, and that Mexico, which is larger and richer than any of her Spanish sisters, is falling behind in the race.

The following table shows how the railways of New Spain and the Mexican portion of it compare

---

* See "Scribner's Monthly" for August, 1877.
† "Life of William Wheelwright" by Alberdi, p. 146.

with those of the United States and the whole world in 1877:

	Mileage.
The whole world	194,836
The United States	77,470
New Spain	6,110
Mexico	378

Yet half of New Spain is within the progressive United States, and the other half is next-door neighbor!

Why this indifference to the demands of civilization, neglect of internal improvements, and disregard of commerce? Why has the country, which produces 75 per cent. of the silver of the world, but $3\frac{13}{100}$ per cent. of the railway mileage of the world? Is nature the cause of this singular condition of affairs, and has she placed barriers to the advance of railways through the Southwest?

FACILITIES FOR BUILDING RAILWAYS IN THE SOUTHWEST.

Whatever barriers nature has placed in the way of progress, in New Spain, are between the coast and interior of Mexico, and not along the great table-lands, for they make the construction of public highways north and south, through the great interior of New Spain, comparatively easy. We have already noticed on previous pages how difficult was the building of the Vera Cruz Railway, and that the highly elevated table-lands, which decline abruptly on the east and west, toward the coast of Mexico, present, most everywhere, similar obstacles to the advance of railways from the oceans; that the Mexicans themselves, in an official report, have recognized and regretted the obstacles to communication between the coast and the interior; how the great interior of New Spain is unlike the great interior of the United States without a river system, and therefore all the more dependent upon railways for its material development and commerce; also how the elevated table-lands which extend from Mexico into the United States gradually slope toward the border line, there find their lowest elevation, and then ascend in the shape of an inclined plain northwardly through New Mexico.* Of the facilities for commercial highways furnished by the table-lands, Humboldt says: " Carriages may run from Mexico to Santa Fé in an extent which exceeds the length which the chain of the Alps would have, if it was prolonged without interruption, from Geneva to the shores of the Black Sea. In fact, the central table-land is traveled in four-wheeled carriages in all directions from the Capital

---

* Ante, pp. 210, 21–25, and 188.

to Guanaxuato, Durango, Chihuahua, Valladolid, Guadalaxara, and Perote." *

In his "Views of Nature," in describing this natural highway along the flattened crest of the mountains between Santa Fé and the City of Mexico, he gives a table of elevations along the line. The two extremities, Mexico and Santa Fé, are respectively 7,469 and 7,047 feet above the sea; but the elevation at El Paso, near the border line, is only 3,810 feet.† This depression in the tablelands extends through their whole width, from east to west, making through the center of New Spain, and at 32° north latitude, near the border between Mexico and the United States, another invitation from nature for the advance of railways. ‡

This idea would appear more clearly on the accompanying map if we had given the elevations according to every thousand feet; but having no data to illustrate, in this manner, the topography of Mexico, it was necessary to give the corresponding elevations for the United States.

Emory's official report on the Mexican Boundary Survey describes the peculiar formation very clearly as follows: "This plateau attains its greatest elevation in Mexico, where it is ten thousand feet

---

* Humboldt's "New Spain," iv., pp. 2 and 3.
† "Views of Nature," p. 208.
‡ Pacific Railway Reports, i., pp. 4 and 5.

above the level of the sea. Its lowest depression is along the line of the boundary, about the parallel of 32° north latitude, where it is about four thousand feet above the sea. Thence it ascends again, and preserves an elevation varying from seven to eight thousand feet to near the 49th parallel."

Again, after mentioning some features of the Sierra Nevada Mountains, he says: "That range, as well as the Sierra Madre and the Rocky Mountains, about the parallel of 32°, lose their continuous character, and assume the forms that are graphically described in the western country as *lost* mountains—that is to say, mountains which have no apparent connection with each other. They preserve, however, their general direction, N. W. and S. E., showing that the upheaving power which produced them was the same, but in a diminished and irregular force. They rise abruptly from the plateau, and disappear as suddenly; and by winding around the bases of these mountains it is possible to pass through the mountain system, in this region, near the parallel of 32°, almost on a level of the plateau, so that if the sea were to rise 4,000 feet above its present level the navigator could cross the continent near the 32d parallel of latitude. He would be on soundings of uniform depth from the Gulf of California to the Pecos

River." . . . "I noticed this remarkable depression in the continent in an exploration made by me in 1846, and called to it the attention of Mr. Buchanan, then Secretary of State; and it was upon this information that he instructed our minister, then negotiating the treaty of Guadalupe Hidalgo, not to take a line north of the 32d parallel of latitude in the boundary between the United States and Mexico."*

Nature has not only done her part to facilitate the material development of the Southwest by making easy the construction of commercial highways through its center, from north to south, and east to west, but she has indicated her intentions in such unmistakable terms that it is a discredit to American enterprise that those channels of trade are not already open and the products and manufactures of the two republics finding a continuous interchange.

She has stored such vast quantites of silver and gold beneath the surface of the great Southwest that it must be artificial, and temporary, instead of natural barriers, that have kept railways from advancing to tap its wealth.

---

* Report on Mexican Boundary, by W. H. Emory, i., pp. 40 and 41.

REASONS WHY RAILWAYS HAVE NOT CROSSED THE SOUTHWEST.

The temporary blockade of the development of New Spain was caused, first, by the lethargic civilization which has possessed that country since the days of the Conquest. It was the Northeast, or New England, which received the progressive civilization that has made such thorough work of developing whatever resources nature placed in their way. Gold was what the Spanish conquerors sought in New Spain, but during a supremacy of three hundred years they unlocked but a small portion of the treasures of the mines. And since the commencement of Mexican supremacy in 1821, less attention has been given to internal improvements, and less thorough has been the development of the resources.

Another temporary barrier to progress in the Southwest since railways advanced across the Mississippi River, was the existence of slavery. The dread on the part of the North of adding strength to that institution placed a blockade upon internal improvements so far south. Fortunately the first century of the republic witnessed the removal of unnatural obstacles to progress in the richest portion of the continent.

A LOOK AHEAD.

The railway builders, or the Anglo-Americans, have gradually extended their thrifty civilization westward, and are now cencentrating their energies near the borders of New Spain, preparatory to intersecting that magnificent land with suitable highways, and making thorough work of its development. A glance at the map shows how, from the north, from the eastern portion of Texas, and from the Pacific coast, railways have been commenced, and are advancing toward the interior and the great mining region. Herein lies the adequate development and prosperity of Mexico, and the rest of New Spain. If the Southwest, during the three hundred and fifty-five years since the conquest by Cortez, has been able, without railways and with no thrifty civilization, to make such a wonderful record in the products of silver and gold, what may we not expect when railways intersect its territory, and open up its latent riches?

The experience of California and Nevada during the past few years, with some of the modern aids to advancement, is an indication of the brilliant development we may expect in the Southwest as a whole.

And with railways will advance the commercial supremacy of the United States.

CONCLUSION.

The study of the Southwest is a series of surprises, whether investigating its yield of silver and gold, the variety of its other resources, its topography and wonderful scenery, its luxuries, or the wealth of its written history. But still greater is the surprise that under a European civilization, for three hundred and fifty-five years, its resources are comparatively undeveloped, its highways unbuilt, and, as a whole, its political power insignificant.

We have seen, in comparing its precious metals with those of the world for the same periods, *that the Southwest, from* 1521 *to* 1876, *produced over one-third of the combined products of silver and gold of the whole world; that its silver product was, from* 1521 *to* 1804, *a trifle less than half of that of the world; from* 1804 *to* 1848, *over half of that of the world; from* 1848 *to* 1868, *half of that of the world; from* 1868 *to* 1876, *but a trifle less than two-thirds of that of the world; and for* 1875, *the last year of the whole period, three-fourths of that of the world.*

Yet its modern development has scarcely commenced.

The first century of the republic of the United

States was largely spent in the formation of a government, the settlement of political principles, the conflict over slavery, the civil war, reconstruction, and finally reconciliation. Happily those questions are disposed of, and the arts of peace, internal improvements, the developments of the resources, the revival of industries are the beginning of a new era and a new policy. Under this policy the Southwest, because of its great natural wealth, becomes conspicuous as the favorite field for operations. And why should it not be the favorite field when it has already produced in silver and gold $4,887,512,-605, or more than double the amount of the national debt at the close of 1876; and more than the total sum invested in all of the railways of the United States, which was estimated to be at the beginning of last year $4,600,000,000.* Yet the Southwest is itself comparatively a stranger to railways.

The Monroe doctrine, which was opposed to the introduction upon this continent of the European system, or forms of government, has become a well-settled policy, and was re-affirmed at the time Maximilian was in power in Mexico, and resulted in the withdrawal of the French troops and his subsequent downfall. But, in marked contrast to this established principle, the business community of the

---

* Poor's Manual of Railways for 1876-7, p. xiii.

United States have ever been content to see England, and France, and other commercial nations of Europe, monopolize the foreign trade of Mexico. Nature intended that trade for this country, and a suitable effort to obtain it must be crowned with success. Already has the tide of American enterprise turned in that direction.

The Southwest is the richest part of the earth's surface in precious metals, the only part of North America in native civilization, the oldest part of America in European civilization, such as it was, yet the last of all to receive a progressive civilization. Its new era of development has opened at a time when modern agencies of civilization and advancement, such as the railway, the telegraph, the most improved mining machinery and agricultural implements, have nearly reached a stage of perfection. And with such aids this rich land is destined to show a record of material development, and wealth, unparalleled by any history yet written.

THE END

www.ingramcontent.com/pod-product-compliance
Lightning Source LLC
Chambersburg PA
CBHW021830230426
43669CB00008B/922